Copyright © 2015 by UI5CN

All rights reserved. No part of this publication may be reproduced d
in any form or by any means, including photocopyin   r
mechanical methods, without the prior written permissio
of brief quotations embodied in critical reviews and
permitted by copyright law. For permission requests,

"Attention: Permissions Coordinator," at the address below.

Rua Aquilino Ribeiro L280,

Pontinha, Lisbon

1675-292 PT

+351-968621883

www.UI5CN.com

1. The main category of the book — COMPUTERS > Enterprise Applications > General

TECHNOLOGY & ENGINEERING.

2. Another subject category — COMPUTERS > Web > Web Services & APIs

First Edition

Go here

Table of content:

1. Introduction and getting familiarized with the environment. 5

1.1 Using Gateway in application 6

1.2 Basic Architecture 7

1.3 Creation of the services 8

1.4 Testing the services before development 14

Summary 24

2. CRUDQ operations and service implementation 25

2.1 What is a CRUD Operation 25

2.2 Query operation 35

2.3 Read operation 39

2.4 Create operation 45

2.5 Update operation 51

2.6 Delete operation 59

Summary 62

3. Integrating with SAP UI5 and deploying app 64

3.1 Basic setup for SAPUI5 CRUD App 64

3.2 Sharing SAPUI5 Project into SAP 79

Summary 85

1. Introduction and getting familiarized with the environment.

In this section, we are going to see how SAP Netweaver Gateway works.
Your SAPUI5 project will be implemented in Eclipse IDE, installed with the SAPUI5 plug-in.

In order to bring data from external applications to your SAPUI5 application, we will be using AJAX calls which will be hitting our SAP OData services.

These services will be responsible for creating, reading or updating any entries in our SAP tables.

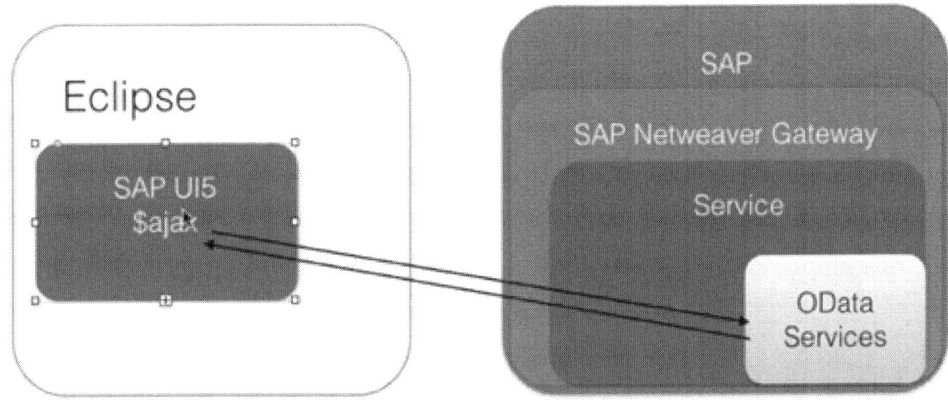

Development Environment

SAP UI5 APP

There is a clear separation between your user interface and your backend infrastructure.

1.1 Using Gateway in application

The majority of the SAPUI5 application will run in their mobile, tablet, or desktop or in any other device they choose to work with; and the SAPUI5 project will be hosted inside your SAP system, in a Production Environment scenario.

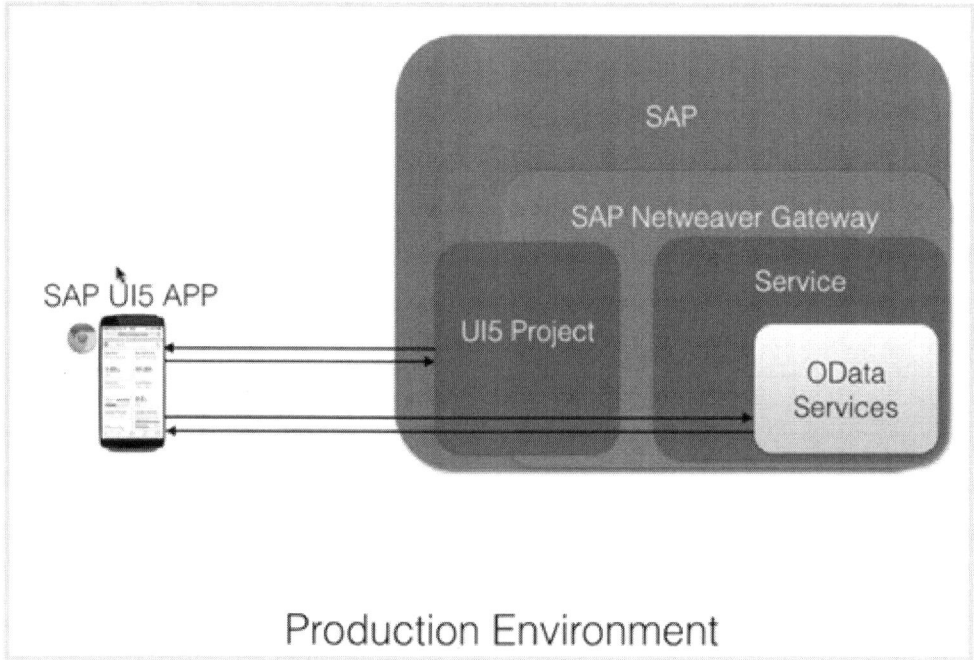

A few parts of your project will host this web application. The web application will be mainly in mobile devices but some parts will be in the server.

In a nutshell, your SAPUI5 application is not a device-specific app like your Android or IOS app, but it is actually a hosted application.

This hosting is done in your server, the SAP Netweaver Gateway server.

SAP Gateway is a web application server like Tomcat or Apache server. It basically hosts your application, your SAPUI5 Project and the application will be running in your client browser or mobile device.

That's how your customer will open the application. Once they open the application, the data communication will be done by your OData services.

This is how the SAPUI5 application will run in your production landscape. All these systems will be actually production systems and your client will be using a web browser to open this UI5 application.

Now, let's see the services and how this SAP Netweaver Gateway is actually configured.

To understand the SAP Netweaver Gateway, we need to answer three questions:
1. How SAP Netweaver Gateway fits into SAP
2. How the service creation is done with the Netweaver Gateway
3. How the testing is done for further development.

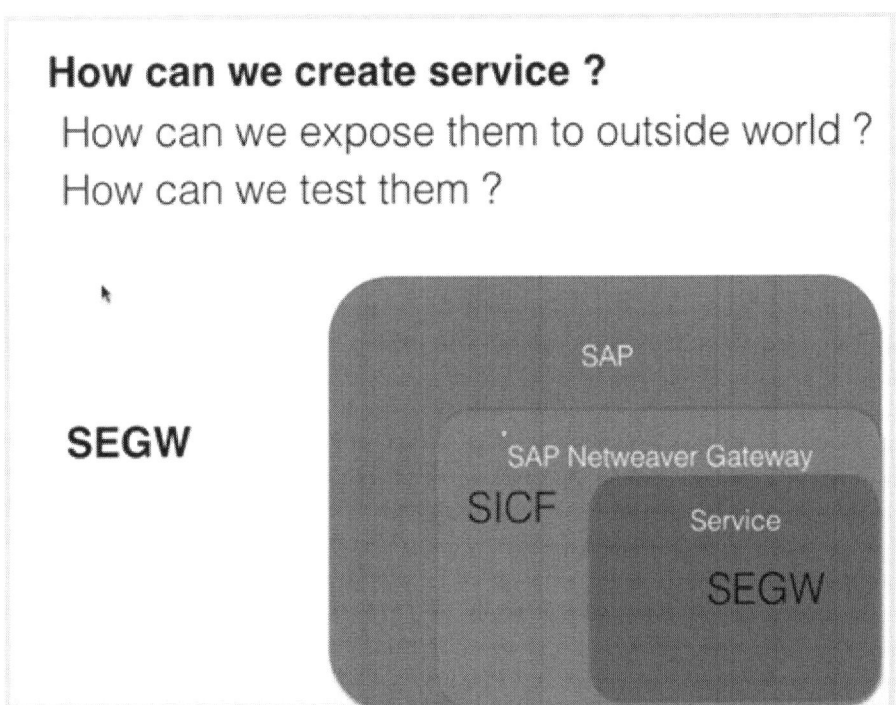

1.2 Basic Architecture

So the first main question which you can ask now is: how can we create the services? These services will be responsible for OData communication, so how can we create them if you want to create a new application?

Second is: how can we expose them to outside world? How can we put them on a web server where anyone can access the data via OData? We will look into the authorizing concept, and the authorization process will be in-built with our services.

The third main question is: how can we test the services that we just created? These are the three main questions which we will be seeing now.

1.3 Creation of the services

We create our services using transaction "SEGW".

> **T-Code: SEGW**
>
> A completely new design-time transaction, which provides developers with an easy-to-use set of tools for creating services. It has been conceived for the code-based oData Channel and supports developers throughout the entire development life cycle of a service.

Let us open our SAP system, and go to "**SEGW**" transaction, the SAP NetWeaver Gateway Service Builder.

As you can see there are many services created here. Let's create one.

Create a project and name the service as "Z_DEMO_TEST3".

Write a description, for example "testing SAP UI5". Give the Package a name. Make it a Local Object.

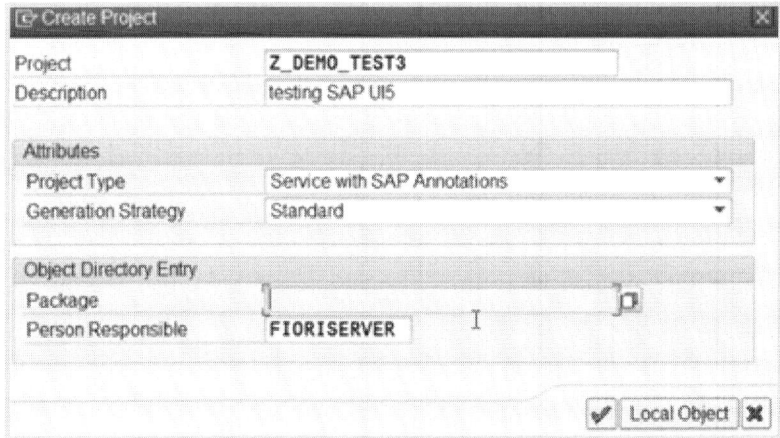

In the end, four folders will get created inside the newly created service:
1. Data Model
2. Service Implementation
3. Runtime Artifacts
4. Service Maintenance

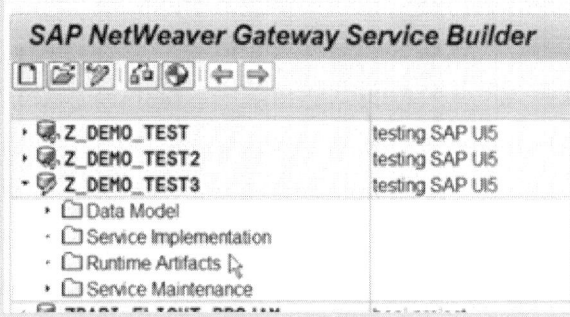

This is the service creation process.

The first thing which we have to do after creating a service is to tell the service what are all the elements or entities which the service will be involved, or what are all the fields that will be read and dealt with the services.

We could automate things by using an RFC or BAPI calls but we will show the manual way, based on custom tables/structures, since usually we don't have interfaces for the custom services that need to be created.

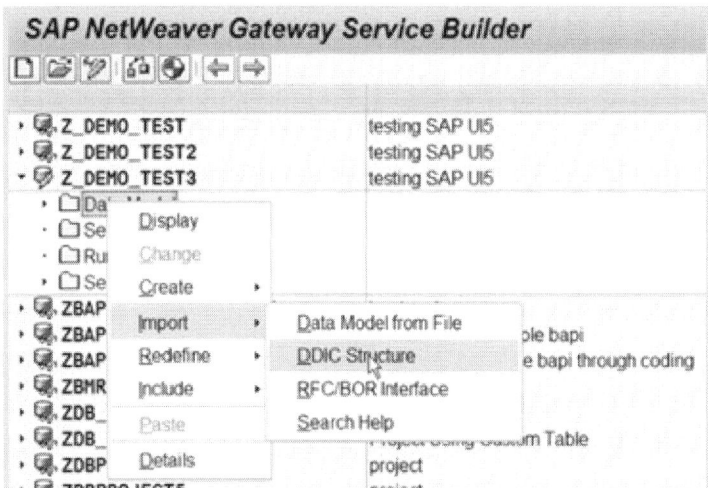

Let's see the structure of a custom table first.

Go to se11 transaction. At the Database table, we type "ZUI5_demo_table". This is a very simple table with five fields and a key.

The five fields are: sales documents number, client, sales document creation date, name of the person who created this and the customer PO number.

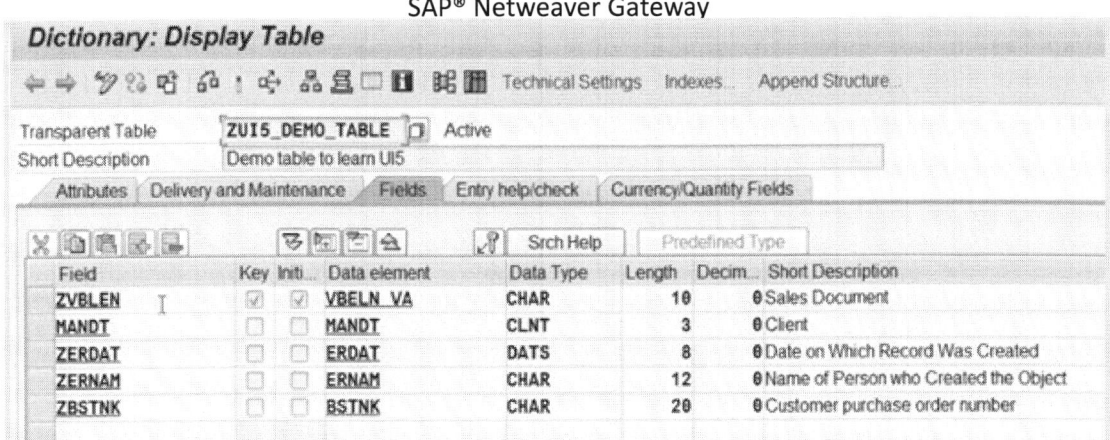

Going back to the SAP NetWeaver Gateway Service Builder, right-click on Data Model and go to Import the DDIC structure.

This is a three-step process.

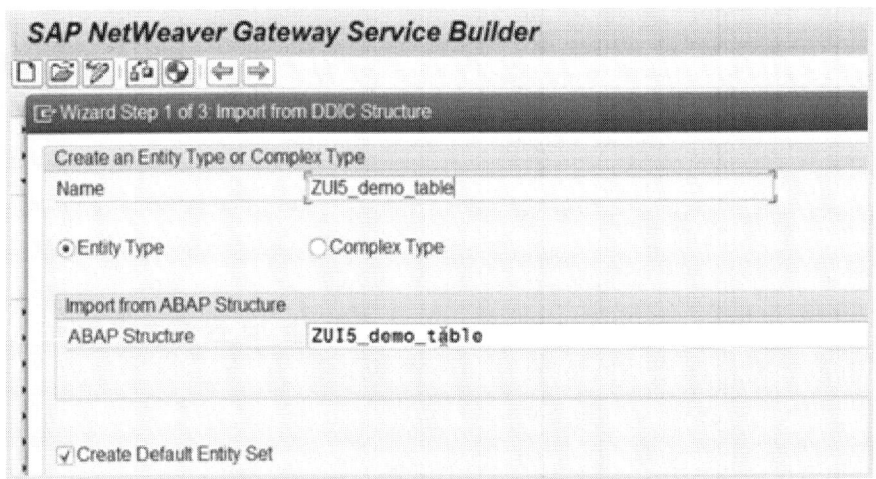

Select "Entity Type" and write the table name, that the service is going to use, in the Name and ABAP Structure fields. Click Next.

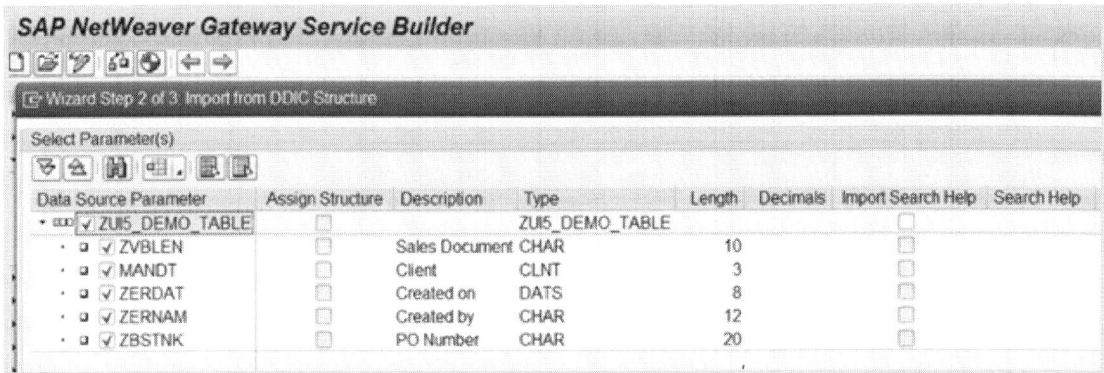

Next, you will be asked for the fields that will be included in the service. Select all of them. Click Next.

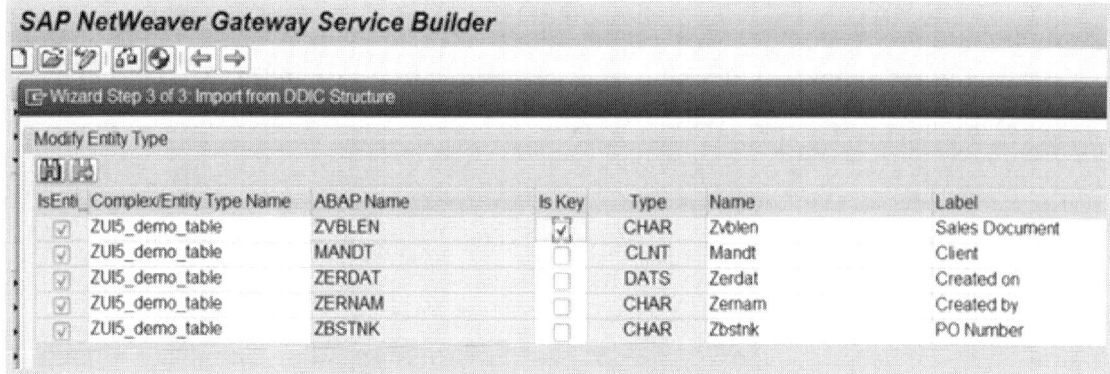

Select the key fields. Make the ZVBLEN as the key. Hit Finish.

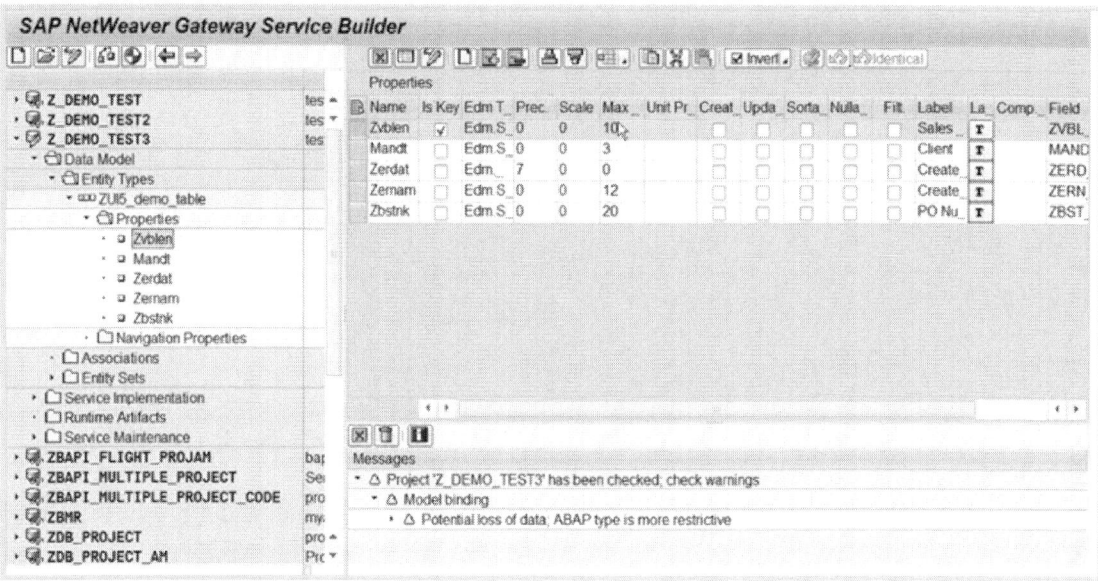

If you expand Data Model, you can see, inside Entity Types, the Properties that were added to the *ZUI5_demo_table* structure and all their details.

When we import these entities from our table, we are telling the service that these are all the fields which will be involved in CRUD operations.

By marking the tick boxes, we say what fields are used/allowed in each specific operation: creation, updating, sorting or filtering.
Save this.
The next step is to generate the provider classes. These are some of the classes that will be generated. We will have to overwrite or implement these classes so

that whenever we are calling the service, the implemented ABAP call will be run and whatever result is returned from those classes or interfaces will be shown in the service response. Make it as a local object.

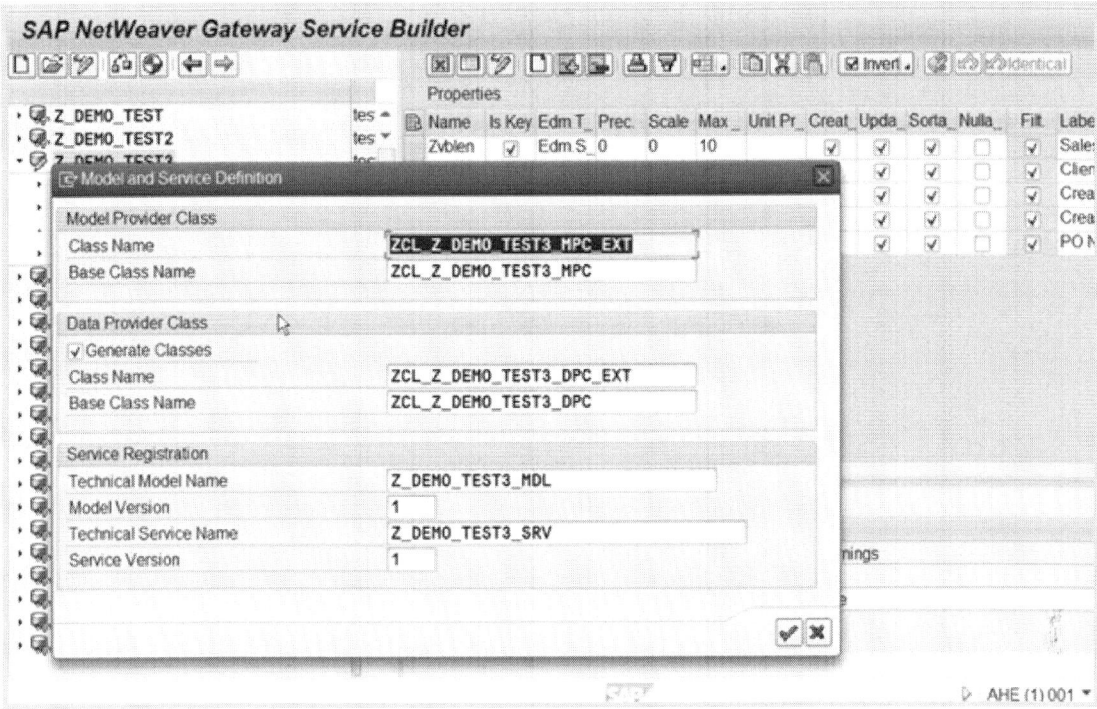

Once we are able to create the service implementation, we can see, inside Runtime Artifacts folder, the new files that have been created.

The DPC stands for the Data Provider Class and the MPC stands for Model Provider Class. We will be implementing the DPC and the MPC.

T-Code : /IWFND/MAINT_SERVICE

This T-Code will be used for the purpose of service maintains, and in recent version, this action can also be done with SEGW transaction.

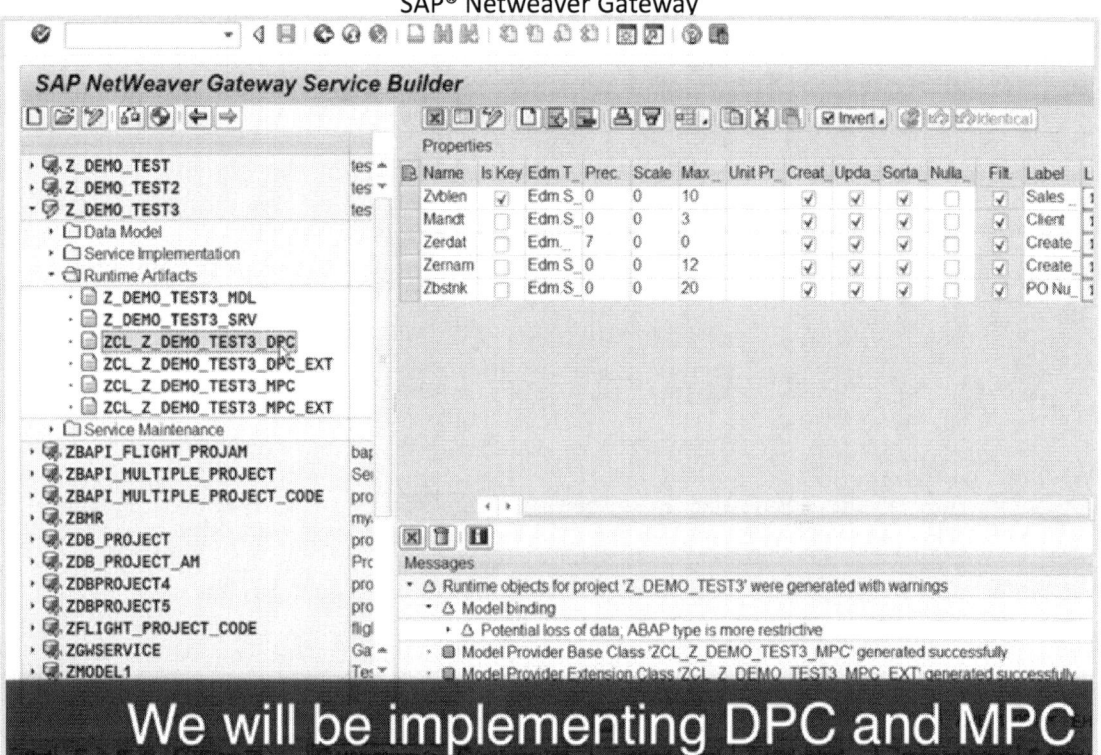

Before doing that, we would like to register the service under Service Maintenance. You can do it afterwards as well, but we will test this service for now.

1.4 Testing the services before development

Technical Service Name is the name of our service. Assign this as a Local Object. Click on Continue.

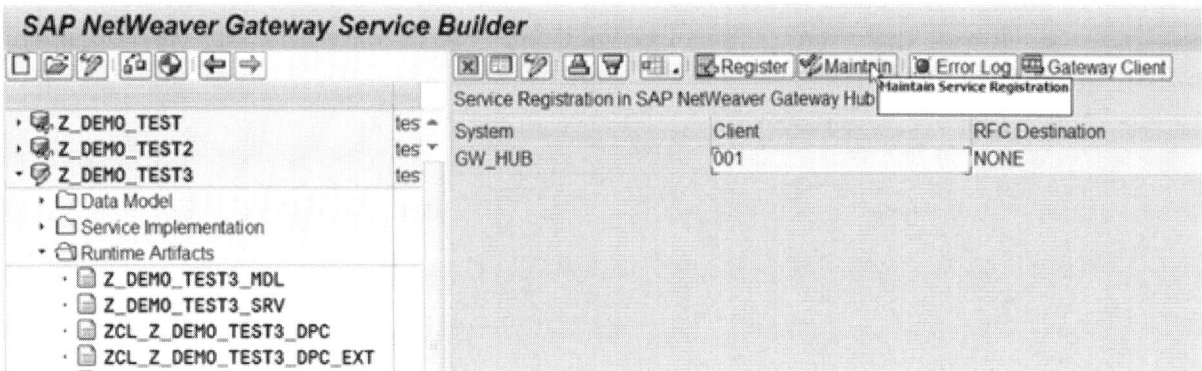

Go to Maintain, which will automatically redirect to the Activate and Maintain Services transaction.

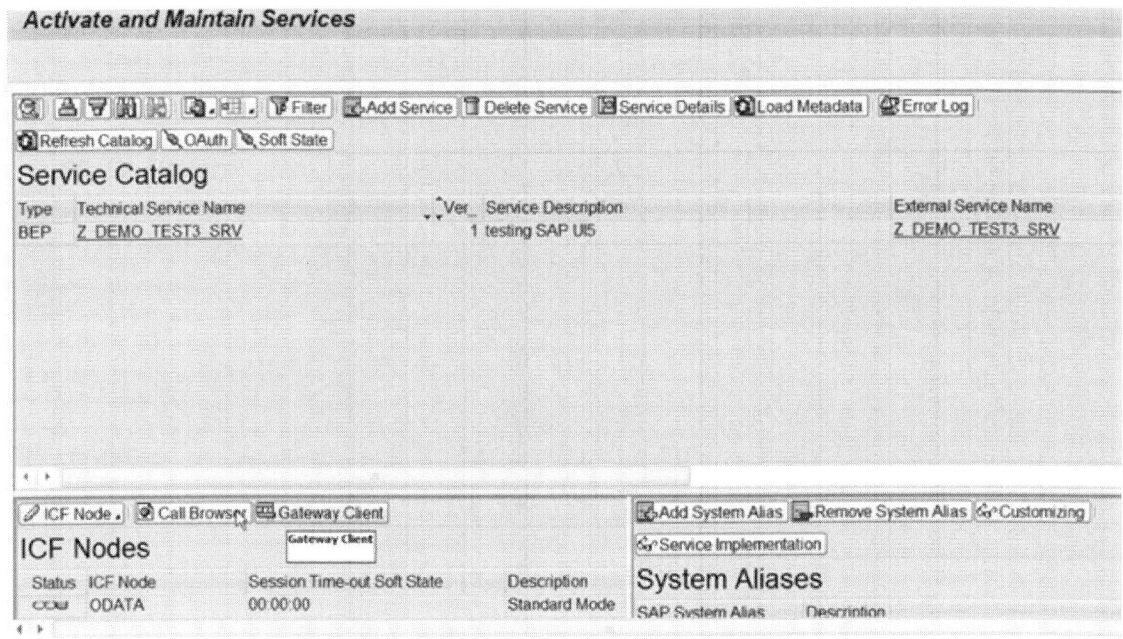

Under ICF Nodes, we can see the status of the service. Green-colored status means this can be reached from outside SAP via web browser.

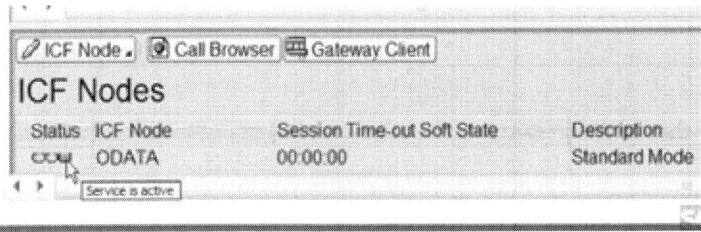

First, we will test with the Gateway Client. Click Execute. Under HTTP Response, you will be able to see some results. The HTTP status code is 200, which is okay.

SAP® Netweaver Gateway

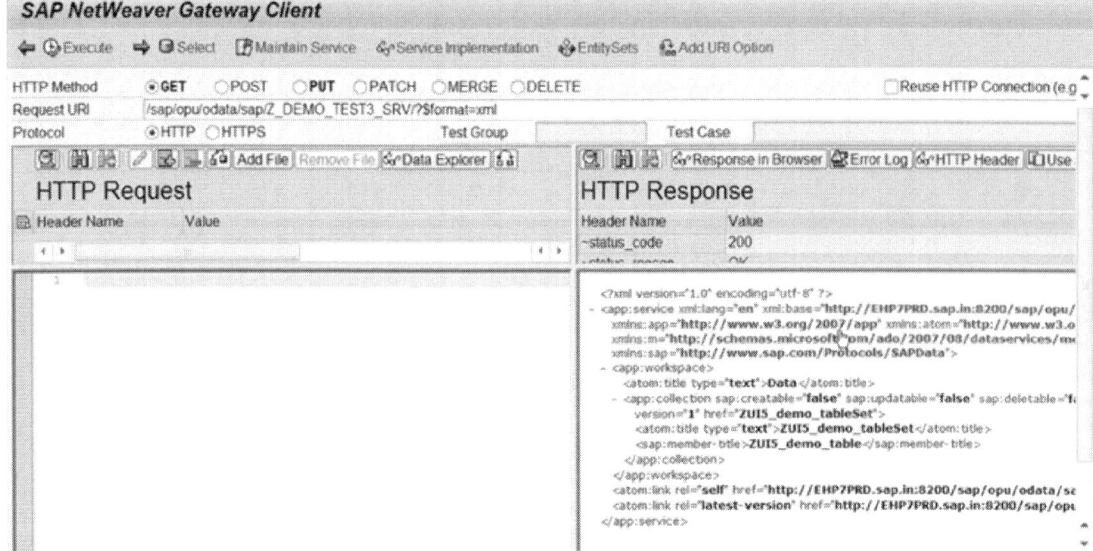

If we change the format to JSON, then it will be more readable, by appending ?$format=json at the end of the URL.

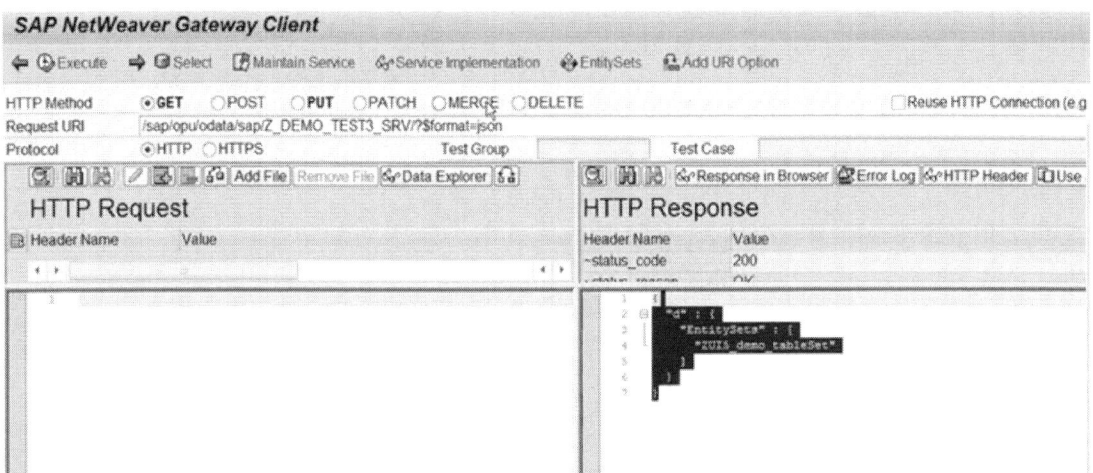

Now, let us do a browser call to show how it looks like in the browser. The SAP system will be asking for credentials. It will not allow to see the service or any data before you give some authentication. Use the username and password of your SAP logon. You can now open this in your web browser, and see the results.

You can also see the metadata information, which will give all the fields involved in the services and basic information by using $metadata keyword after service name.

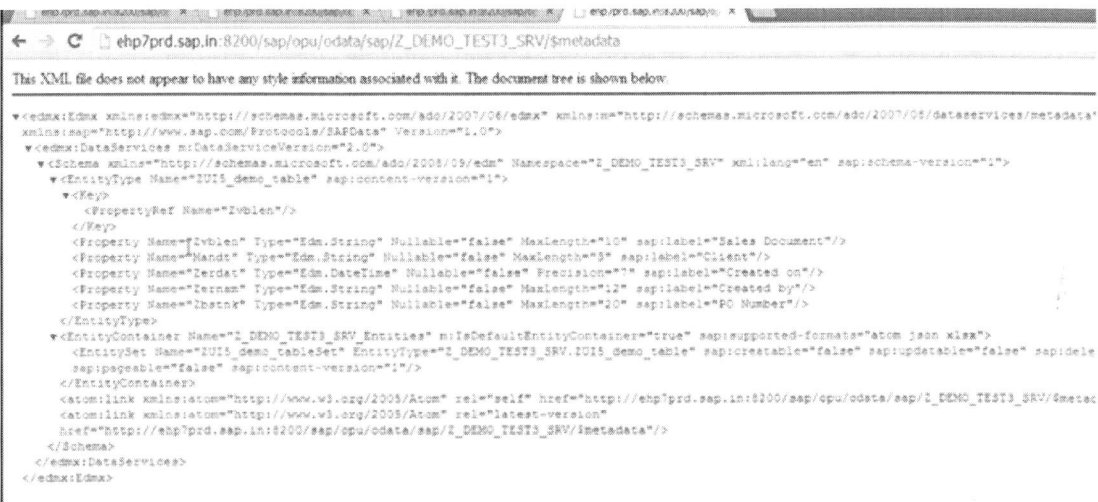

Going back and reviewing what we have done so far: we created our services. We told the services what are the data elements and entities which will be involved in the services. We directly imported all entities from our Z structure. We registered the service, and then we checked if everything was working or not.

We have also seen the SEGW transaction where we are creating our services.

How can we create service ?
How can we expose them to outside world ?
How can we test them ?

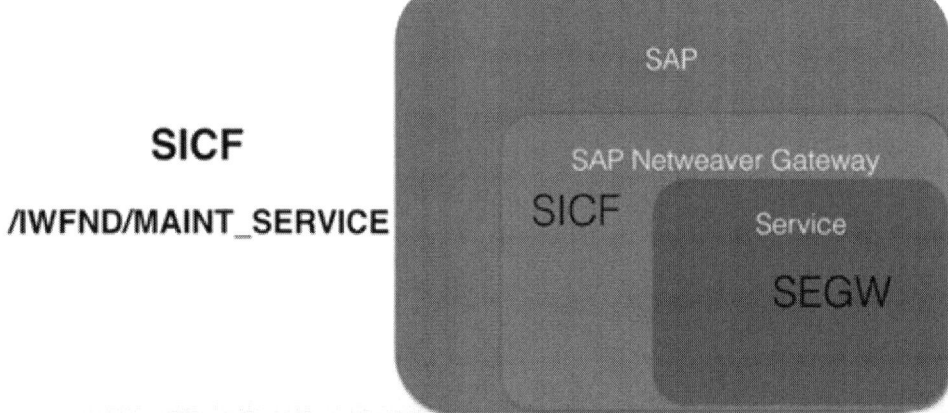

When you want to tell your SAP system how to expose your services to the outside world, then we use the SICF transaction. If you have already done some web application development in SAP, you might have seen SICF transaction, where you maintain all services present in your SAP system.

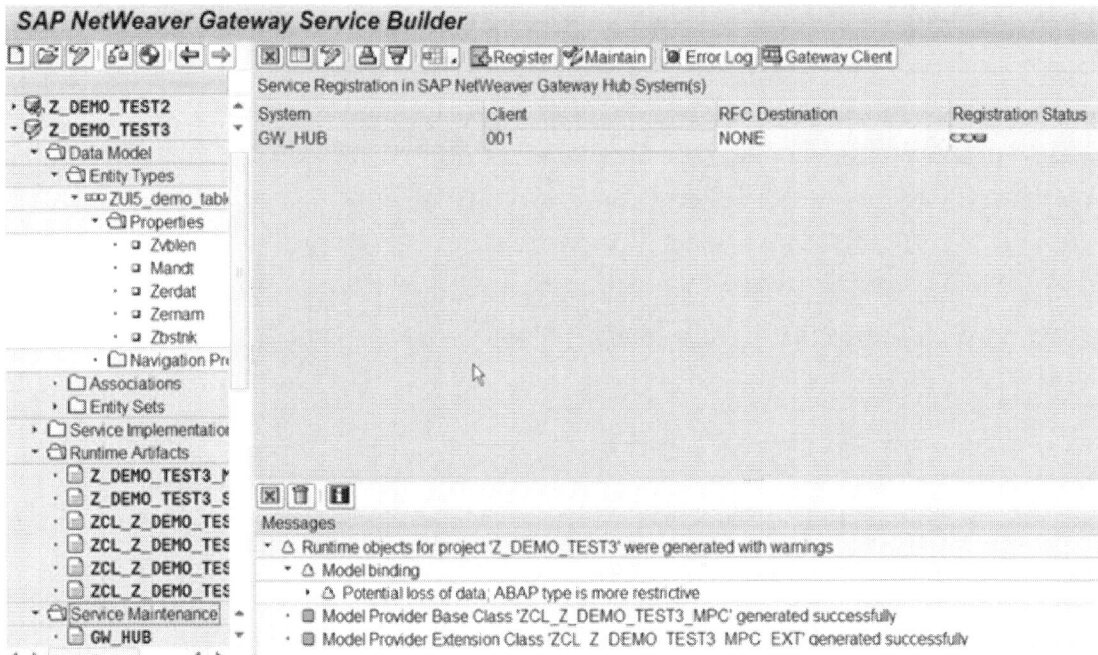

Let us open sicf T-Code. Under Service Name, search for Z_*. You can see that there are services, some activated and some deactivated.

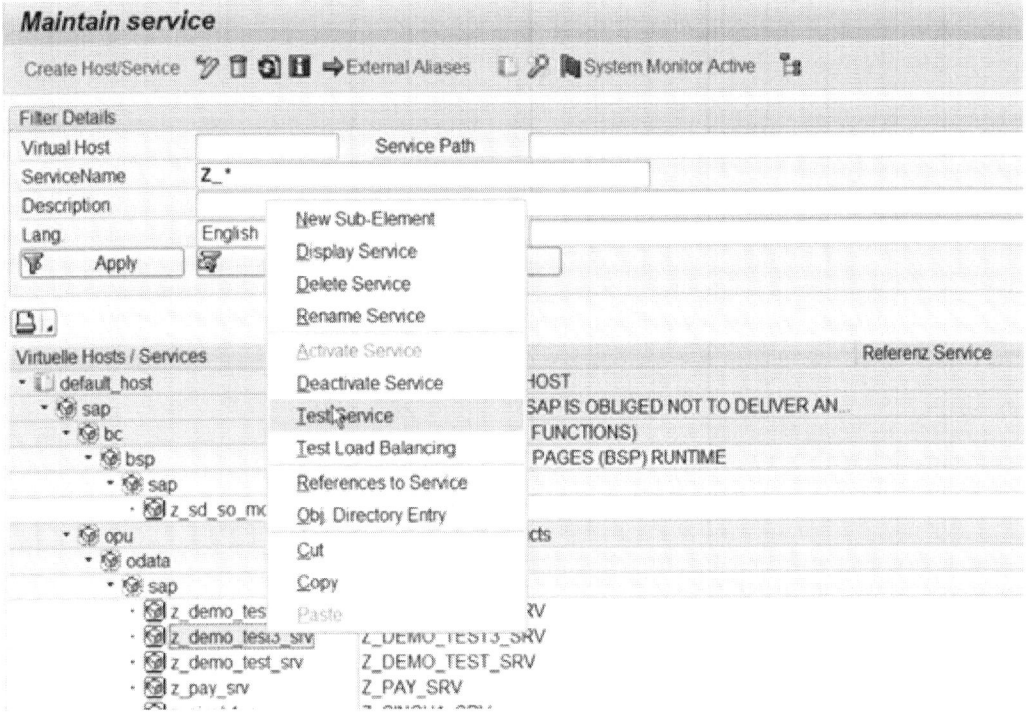

Z_DEMO_TEST3_SRV is activated because we previously went inside the SEGW Service Maintenance folder and directly registered and activated our services. We don't have to go to SICF to do that, but we can still go to the SICF transaction to activate and deactivate your services. If we deactivate the service, then the service will not run.

Now, we can also test the service directly from SICF, and this will ask to open it in the web browser.

One more transaction which you will be seeing is the Service Maintenance transaction.

This transaction code /IWFND/MAINT_SERVICE opens your service maintenance screen where you can see all the services present in the system. But when we go via the shortcut, we are directly shown our own services.

SAP® Netweaver Gateway

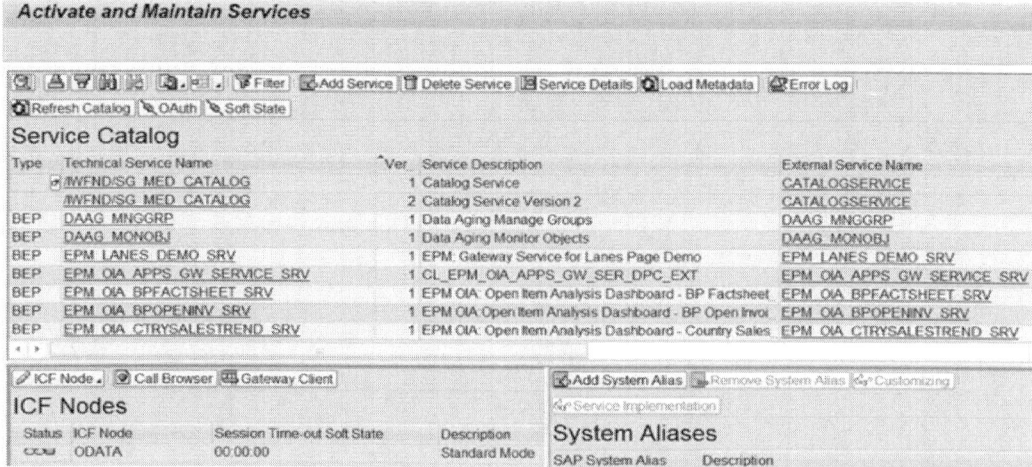

This is the basic maintenance screen which will be used to do all kinds of applications. We can deactivate the ICF node, which will stop our service; we can go to the Gateway client (also referred to as SAP internal browser) to test our services; we can add new services and new system aliases; and, we can see the error logs which are important when we are developing the services, as we will also have some issues to fix.

Now let's go into the part where we will be actually doing some of the operations with our services.

For now, in the web browser, all you can see is the metadata and the basic service information. The first thing we want to do is to implement the class.

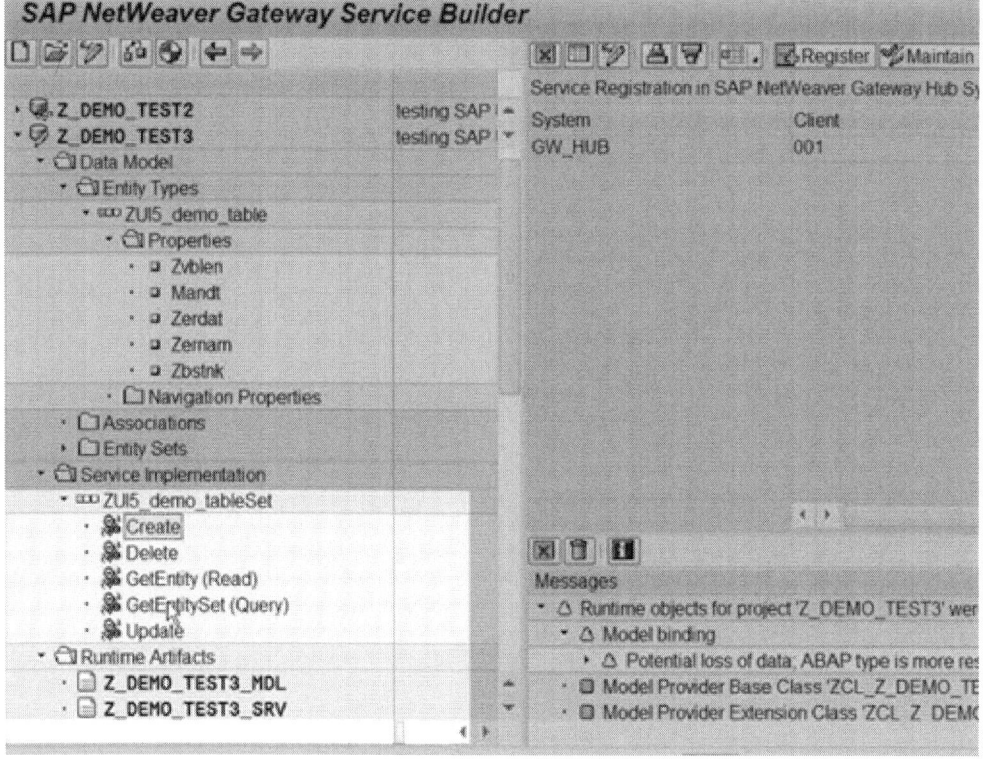

In the SAP Netweaver Gateway Service Builder, if you go inside the Service Implementation folder *ZUI5_demo_tableSet*, you will see all CRUD operations. The CRUD operation is very popular and it covers four parts: creating, reading, updating and deleting your entries from SAP.

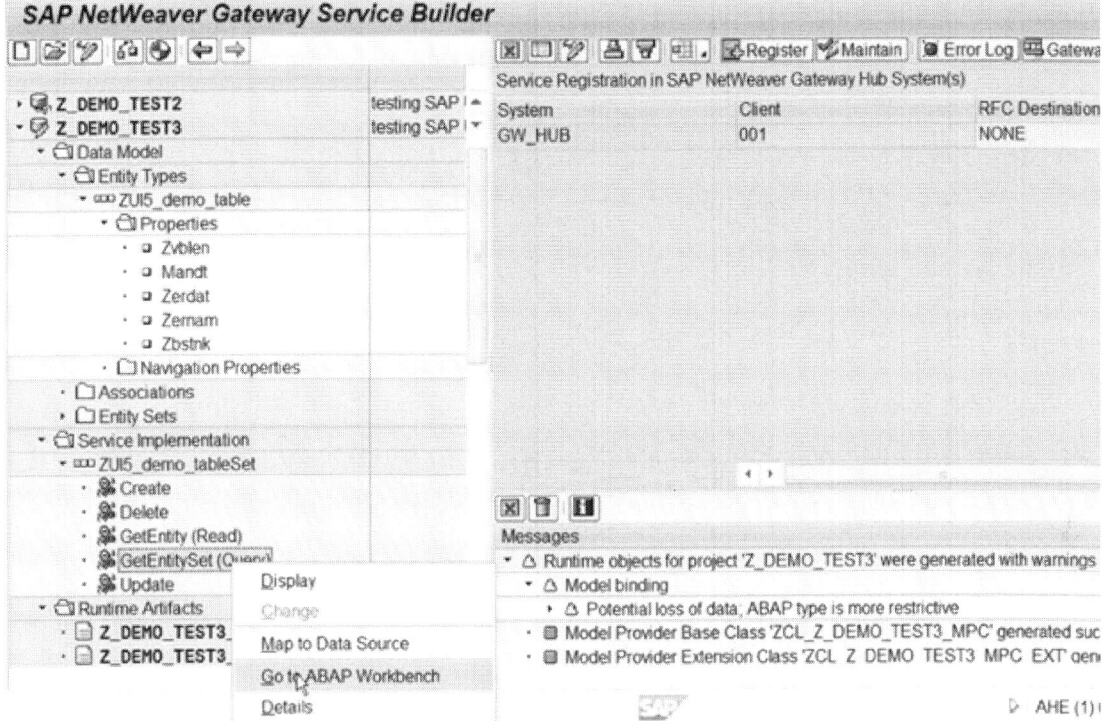

Let us first implement the GetEntitySet.

It is like a SELECT *, it will give all results from your table with all of the fields you have defined. Right-click on *GetEntitySet*, and Go to ABAP Workbench. Save the project.

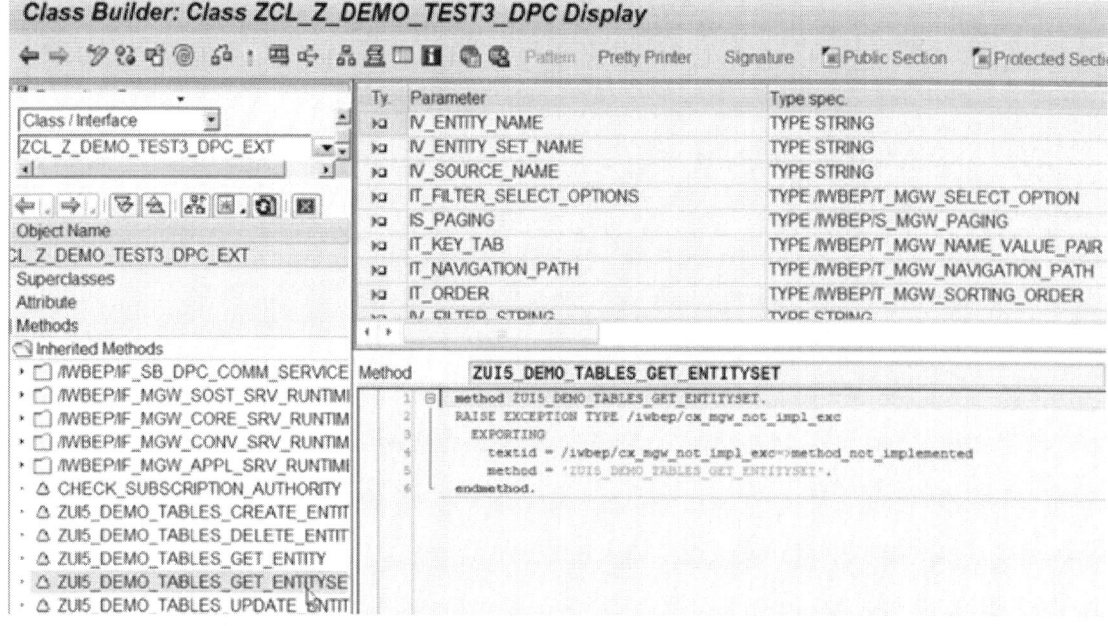

In the Class Builder, we have to navigate inside Methods, then Inherited Methods, and we will see the *GetEntitySet*. Right-click on *GetEntitySet* then Redefine, and it will open this method in edit mode.

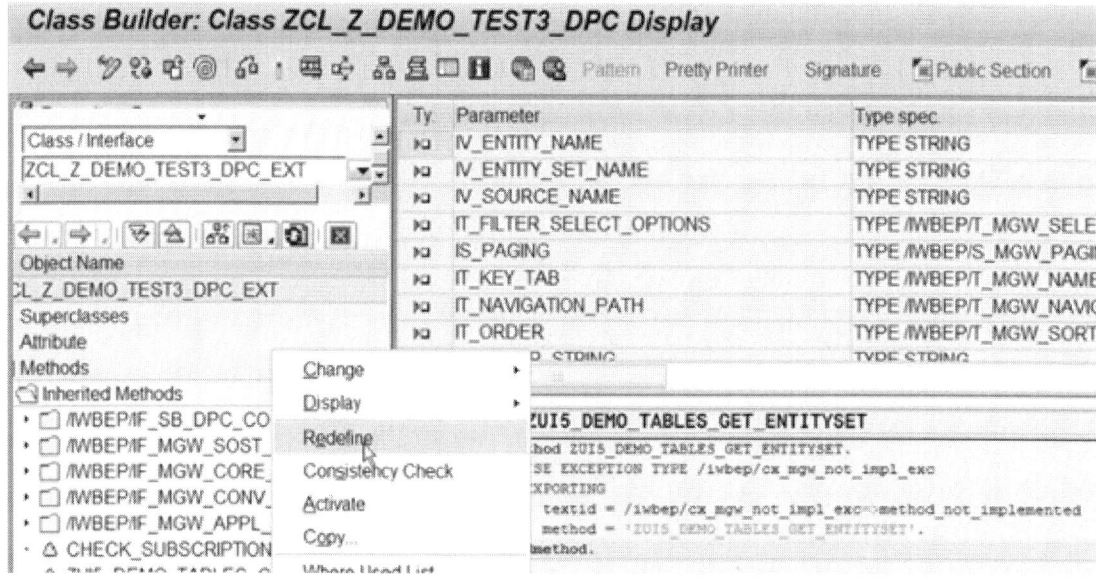

You can see some import parameters, which have been imported by this method, and other two export parameters, which are basically the exceptions.

There are many imported parameters from where you can pass some of the filtering criteria, but the main focus and attention should be at the *ET_ENTITYSET*.

It will be returned by this method, and whatever information *ET_ENTITYSET* will be having, it will be shown in your web browser once your service is returned. In a simple way, *ET_ENTITYSET* will be your body of the response.

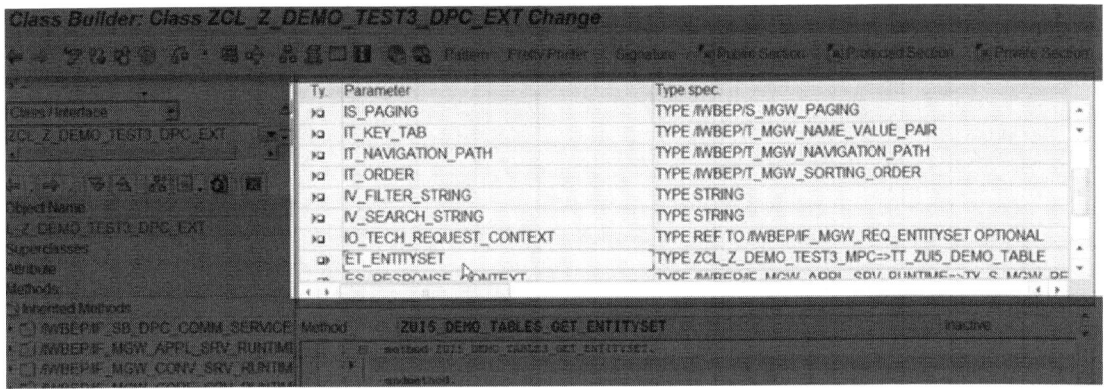

Let's try to implement ET_ENTITYSET for now. We will do a very basic SELECT *:

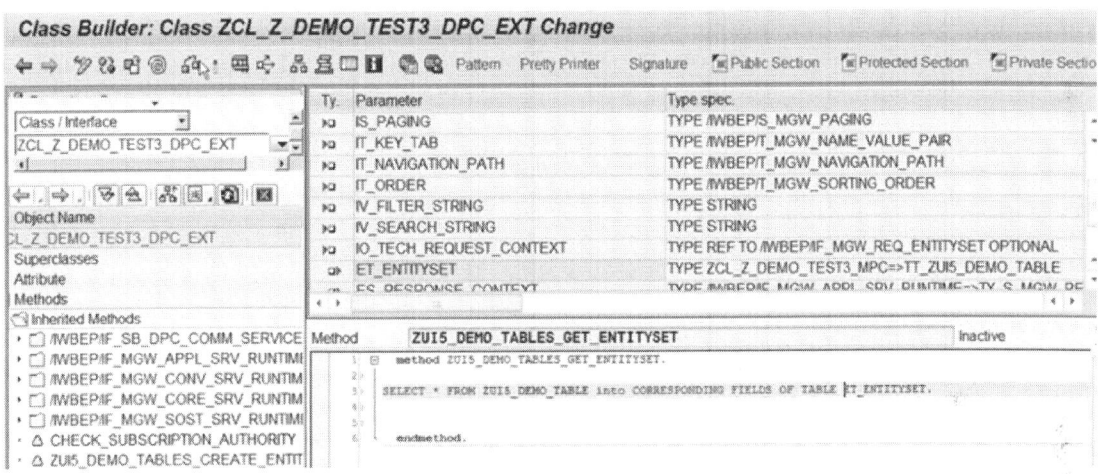

*SELECT * FROM ZUI5_DEMO_TABLE into CORRESPONDING FIELDS OF TABLE ET_ENTITYSET*

Save it and check if things are correct. Activate all of the objects which are selected.

Now, you have your activated object created.

In your web browser, if you open ZUI5_demo_tableSet, you can see the data. This might gives a little relief to see that you are on right track.

Let us showcase this in a very nice JSON format, and you can see that the data which is in your SAP tables is being shown in the web browser.

Basically your UI5 application will be doing your AJAX calls, and they will be getting these JSON objects and show them or do anything they want to do in the UI5.

This is the basic *GetEntitySet* which will be a kind of SELECT *. You can also pass filter criteria here, and get specific entries or results by the key field. You've also seen the $top and $skip in the OData queries. We will also be able to do these operations with our services.

You have to understand that all this is actually done by our ABAP code. You need to write the code in the Class Builder if you want to implement some feature. For example: $top=2, so that you will only see two records.

Here, it's giving four records, because we have not implemented the top feature. We would have to give this logic or build this understanding in our ABAP code to deal with top or filtering criteria. We will be getting all that information of what the URL has through these imported parameters. We will be populating our ET_ENTITYSET table, and whatever the final response is there in the table will be shown in the web browser

In the next section, we will be seeing more of service implementation. Hope that creating, registering and activating the services, as well as basic implementation and testing the *GetEntitySet* are clear to you now.

Summary

In this section, we saw the architecture of SAP NetWeaver Gateway system and how we need to utilize our SAP NetWeaver Gateway system to build application on top of it. Then, we saw how UI5 is using SAP NetWeaver Gateway system.

We came to know three main questions which need to be understood to start Gateway development. Those questions are:
1. How can we create services?
2. How can we expose them to outside world?
3. How can we test them?

To look for the answer, we went inside the Gateway system to know how it is structured. We also understood all the details we have to consider while building a service, like knowing the transaction codes; seeing how a basic service is created and exposed, and how they are accessed from the internet; and, what, as a developer, we have to do to build those services.

At the end, we implemented our first service where we were able to read multiple records of an SAP table.

You can also, check our SAPNetweaver Gateway course which demonstrates all the above steps in simple and easy to understand manner.

For the course coupon click here or use the QR code.

SAP Netweaver Gateway for SAPUI5, SAP Fiori and SAP HANA
UI5 Community Network , SAP Experts - SAP Services, SAP Consulting, SAP Education
20 € · ★★★★☆ 4.2 (25 ratings) • 27 lectures, 3.5 hours video • All Levels

2. CRUDQ operations and service implementation

In this section, we are going to see CRUD operation with SAP NetWeaver Gateway.

2.1 What is a CRUD Operation

Sometimes, it is also referred as CRUDQ. Basically, CRUD stands for Create-Read-Update-Delete, and Q stands for Query.

C.R.U.D.Q
C:Create
R:Read
U:Update
D:Delete
Q:Query

For example, this is your backend table.

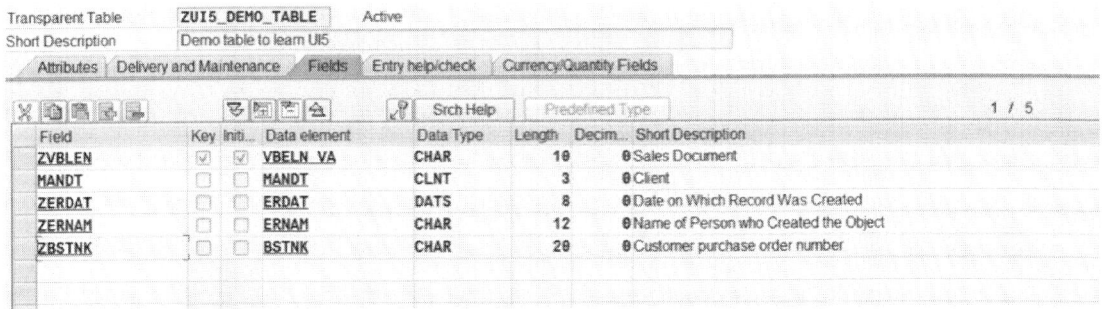

Demo Table created for experiments

In your SAP UI5 application, you are going to use AJAX calls. Via AJAX calls, you are going to maintain backend data and information

For example, you have to maintain this table. What kind of functionality do you require? First of all, you can create, update, and read some records based on some key column inputs or key value inputs.

You can also read the entire records, like the SELECT * operation. You can also delete some of the records. These are all the functionalities which you could require to maintain a single backend table or multiple sets of a backend table, and all of them will be exposed via your Gateway services.

You will be using normal AJAX calls to create, read, update, delete or query records. We implement this CRUD operation in the Gateway so that those backend functionalities are available to your UI5 application via AJAX calls.

So let's see how to do it.

Let us go to SE11 so we can show the table on which we are going to do the operation. The table is *ZUI5_DEMO_TABLE*, and Display the content.

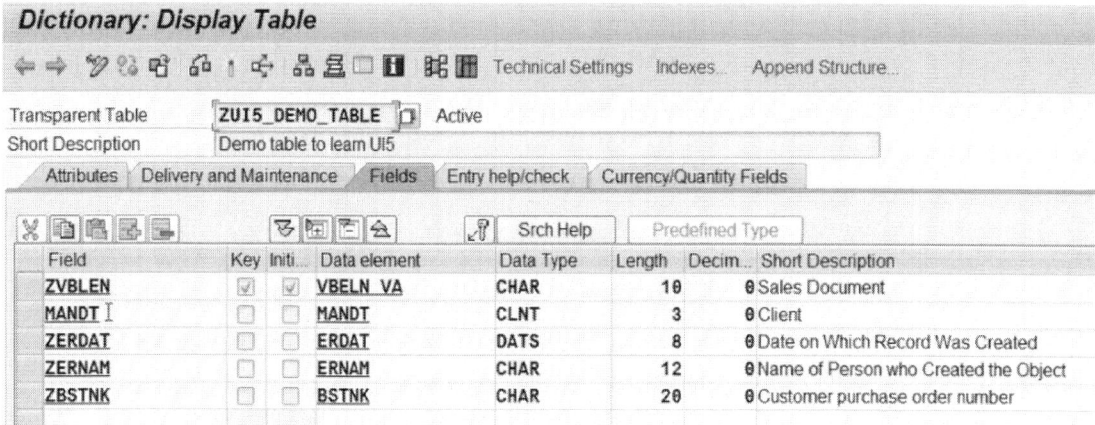

It has five columns. One of them is Client which specifies which client we are in. If we see the records, there are four records created by our services that can be updated and read.

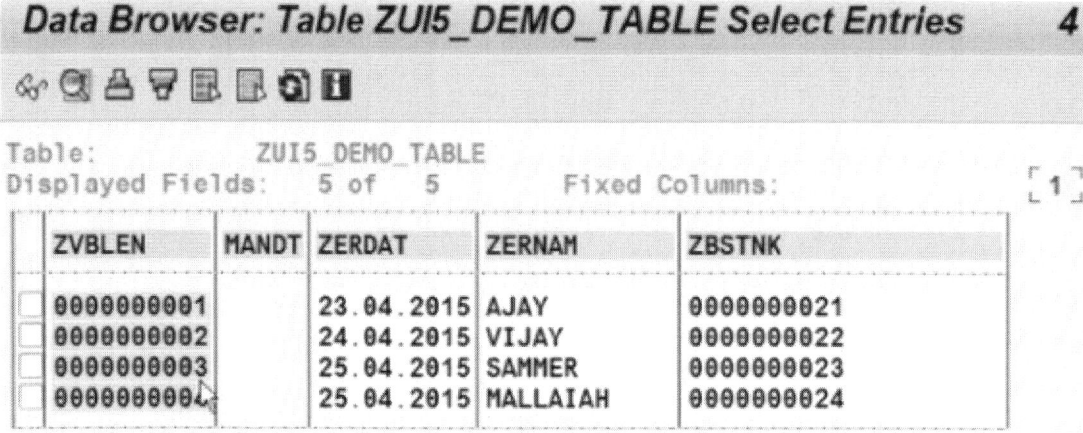

Now let's see how those operations can be done via your Gateway.

To go into the Gateway, go into the SEGW transaction. Create a new service, for example: *Z_DEMO_TEST4*. Put in the description: *demo for recording*. The package can be given as $TMP. If there is no package, you can either write it down or just click on the Local Object. Click on the check button.

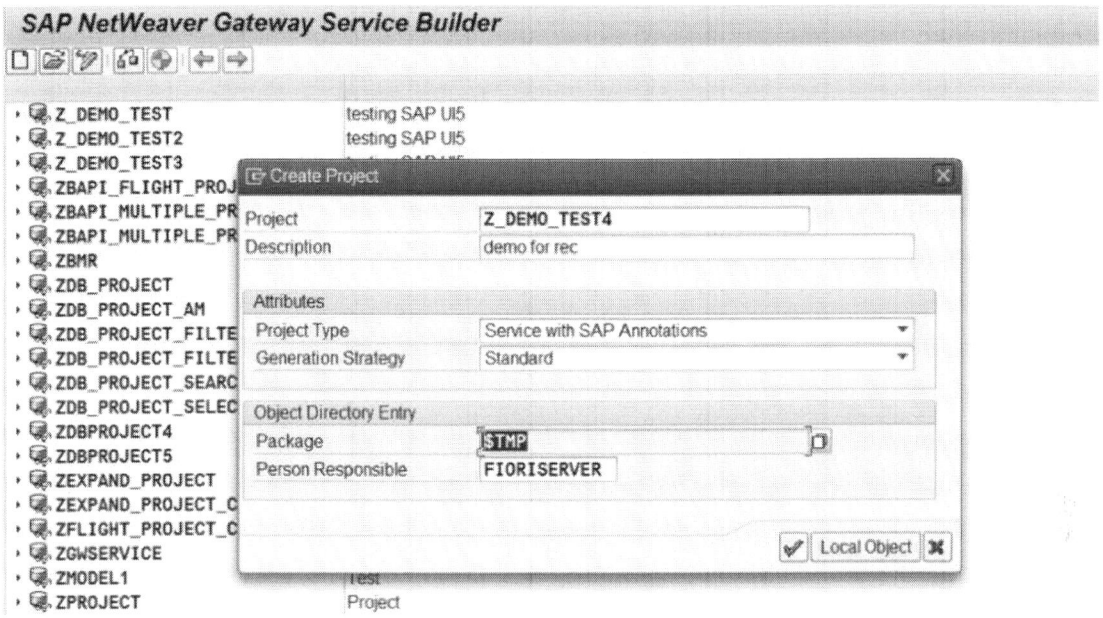

It has created the project to implement the services. You can save this, or you might lose the data if you go into some other transaction. The first step after saving is to import the structure with which your service will be dealing. We will be also working with the table structure which was just showed to you: *ZUI5_demo_table*.

SAP® Netweaver Gateway

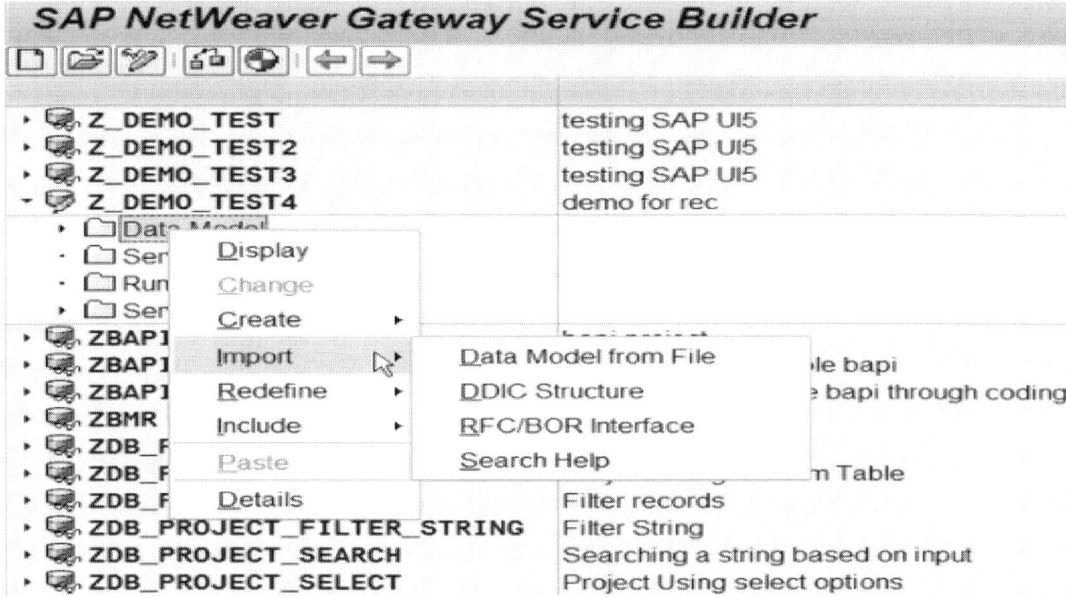

Put in the Entity Name as well. These names can be different, but we're making it the same so it would be easy for us to recognize it in our implementations. Go next.

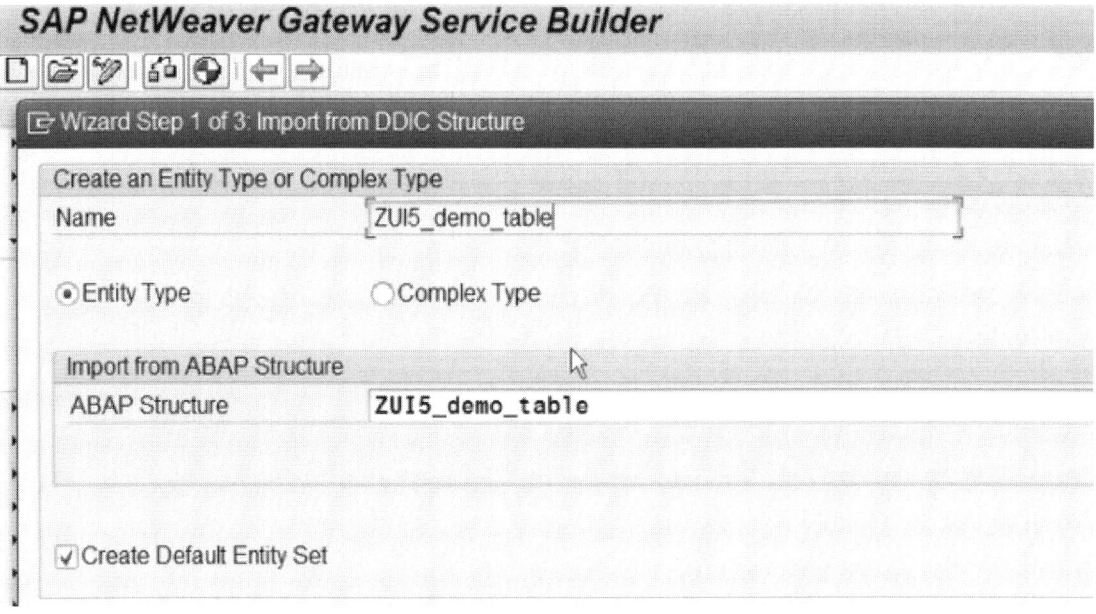

Select all parameters, and click Next.

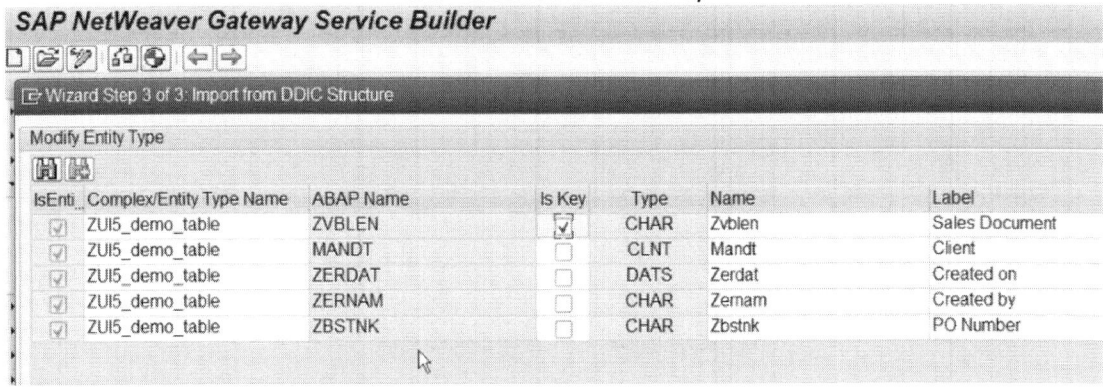

We have to mention which is the key field: ZVBLEN. This table may not have some functional sense or may not be functionally accurate, as this table structure was just created so that you can understand how to implement CRUD operation for now. Hit Finish, and Save.

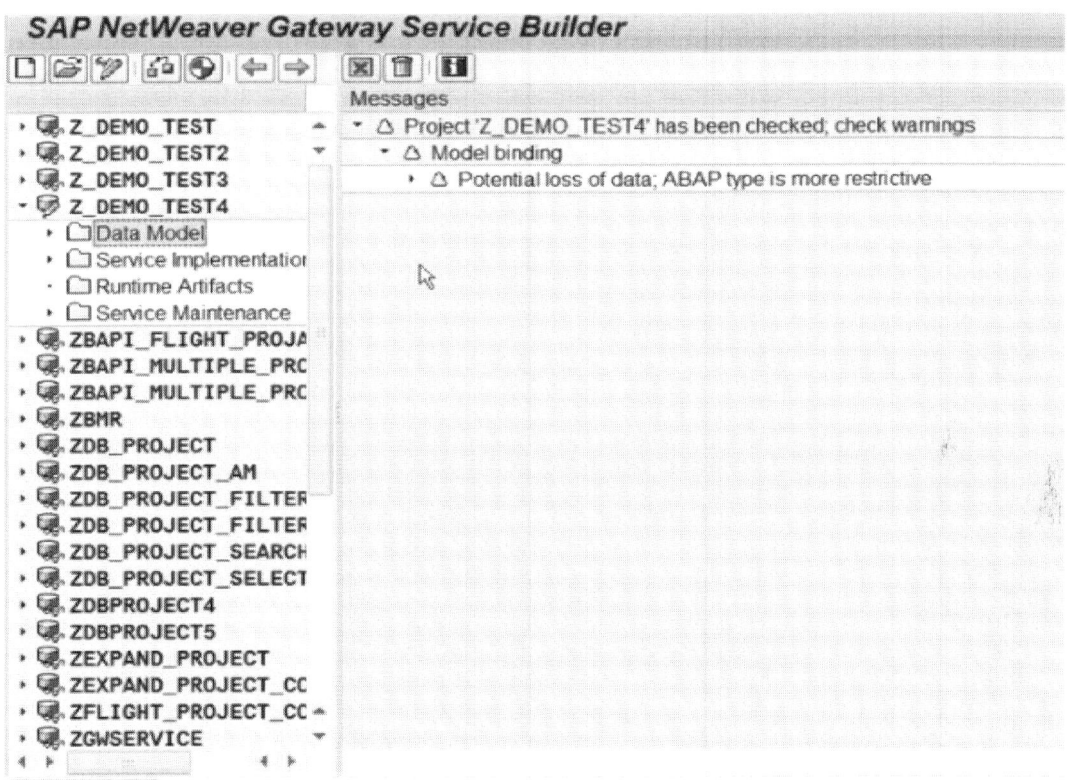

We have imported the structure which will be used by the services. Under Data Model, if you click inside Entity Types, we can see the structure, in which you can see its individual properties.

SAP® Netweaver Gateway

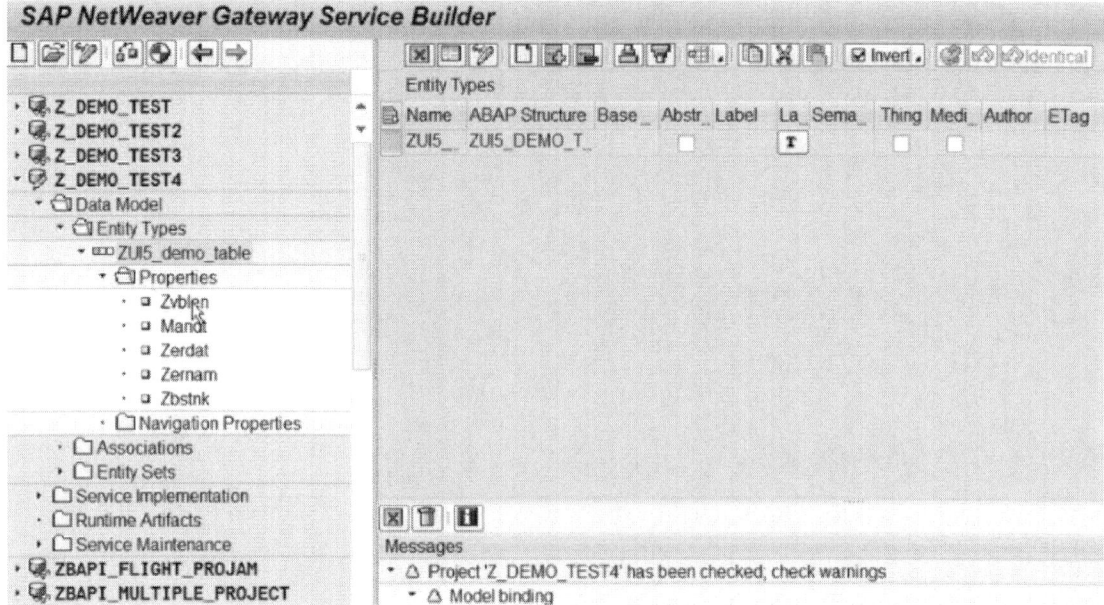

Select all of these, and click Invert. You are saying to your Gateway service that you will be requiring the create operation for all of these entities. They can be created and updated.

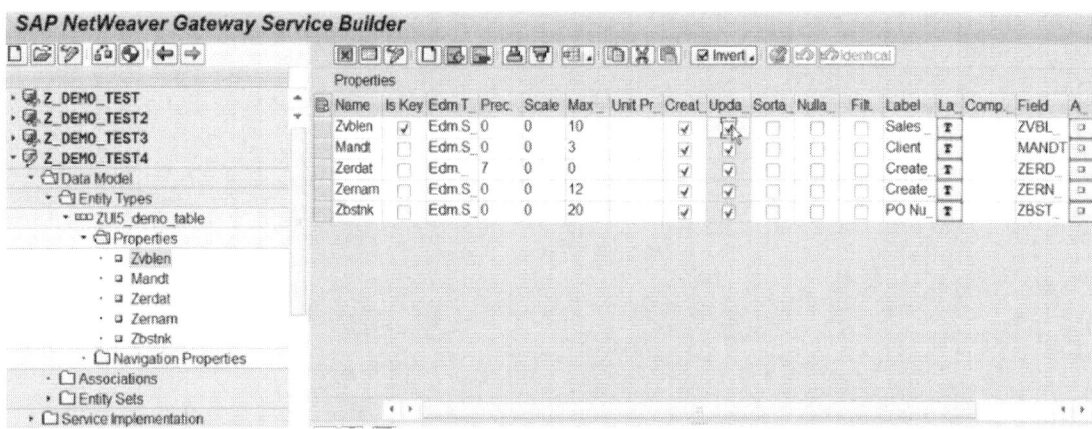

The third step is to go to the project, and Generate Runtime Objects. It will generate the Model Provider Class, and Data Provider Class. We will be implementing DPC, so that we will be getting the data from our services via our AJAX calls which you will use in your UI5 application.

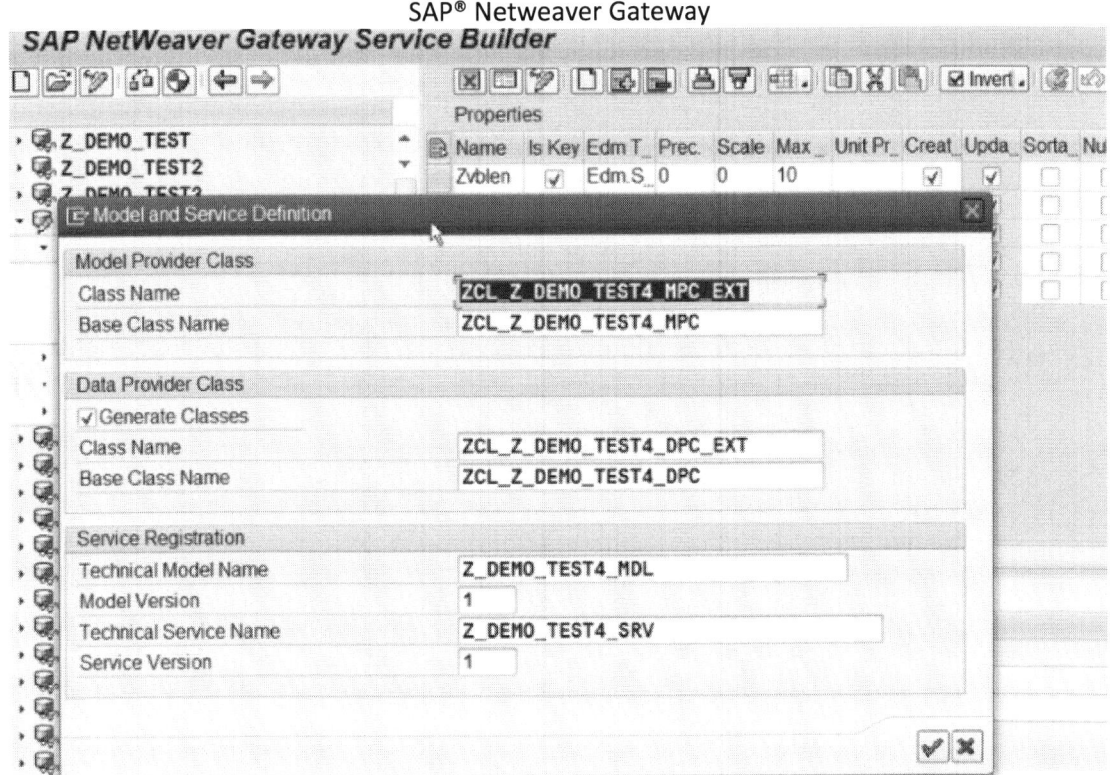

Make this as a local object.

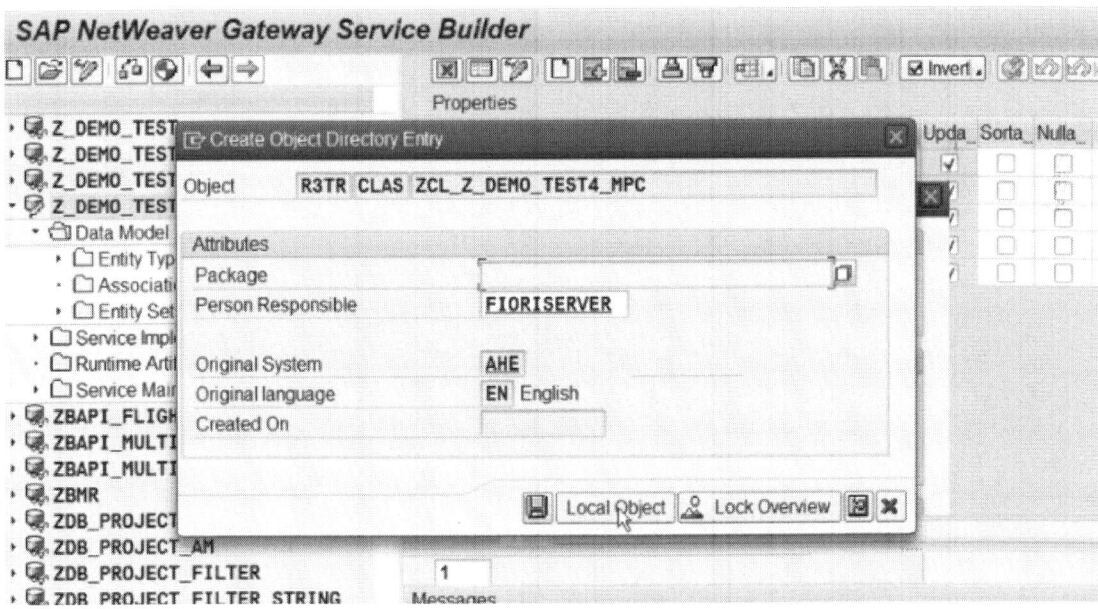

Now that the runtime objects are generated, if you go inside Runtime Artifacts, you will see that both DPC and DPC extensions have been created, as well as MPC and MPC extensions.

We have to focus on DPC because when you query your services from your browsers, the data which you will be getting will be actually given to you by the ABAP syntax which you are going to write, and this is done by the DPC.

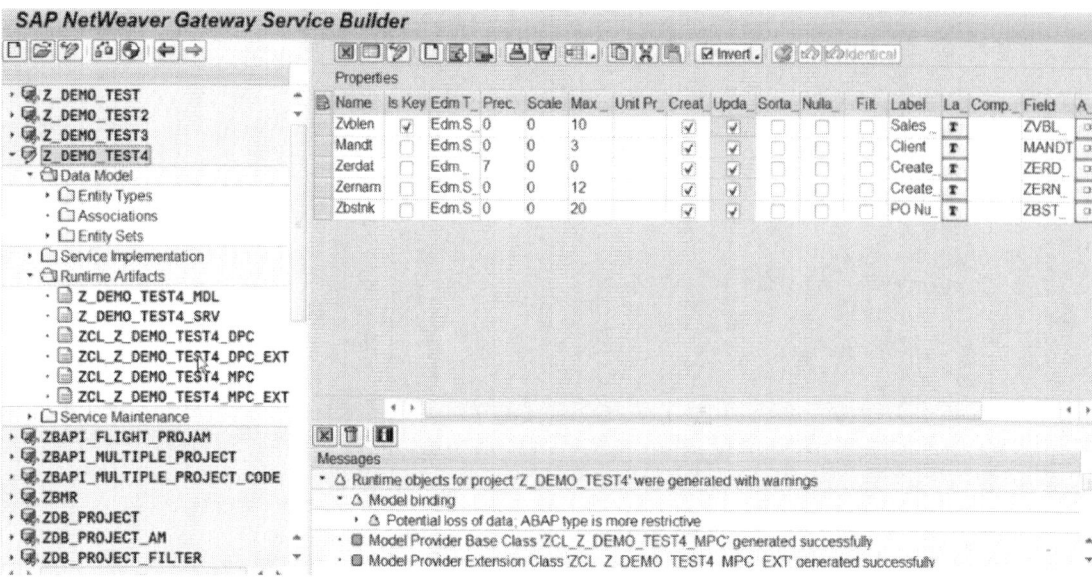

The next thing to do is go to the Gateway Hub, and register your service. This is giving us the description of what will be the service name and more details. Select Local Object, and it will automatically fill-in $TMP in the Package Assignment.

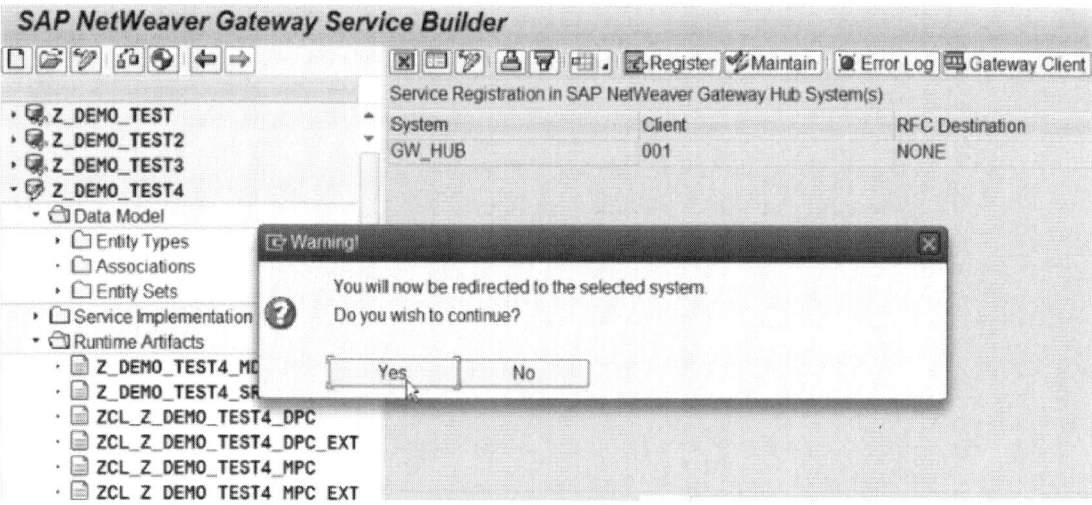

Save and continue.

SAP® Netweaver Gateway

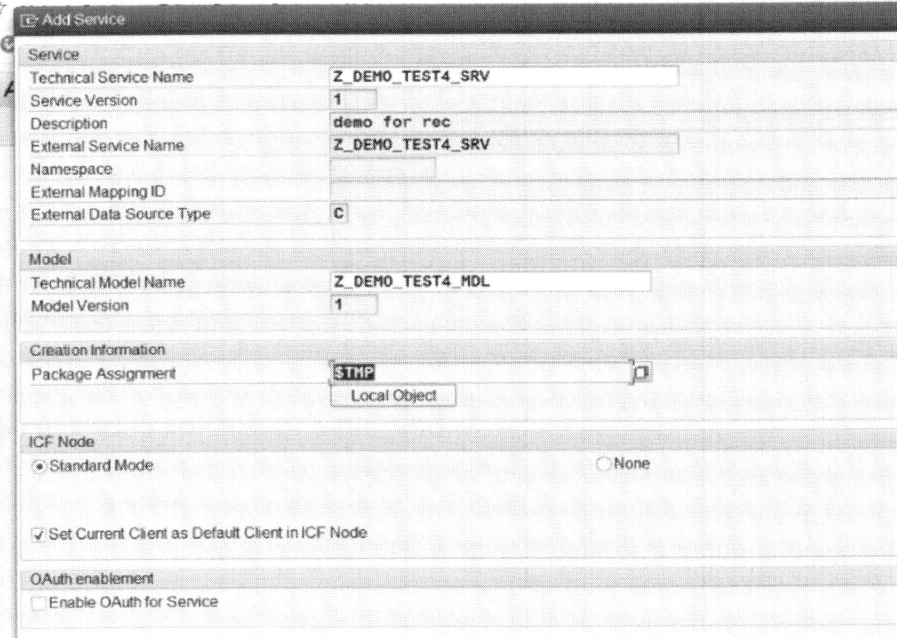

Now that you have registered your service, you can go directly on maintenance and see if the service is running fine. The service has been automatically selected, and you can see that the OData node is active as the status is green.

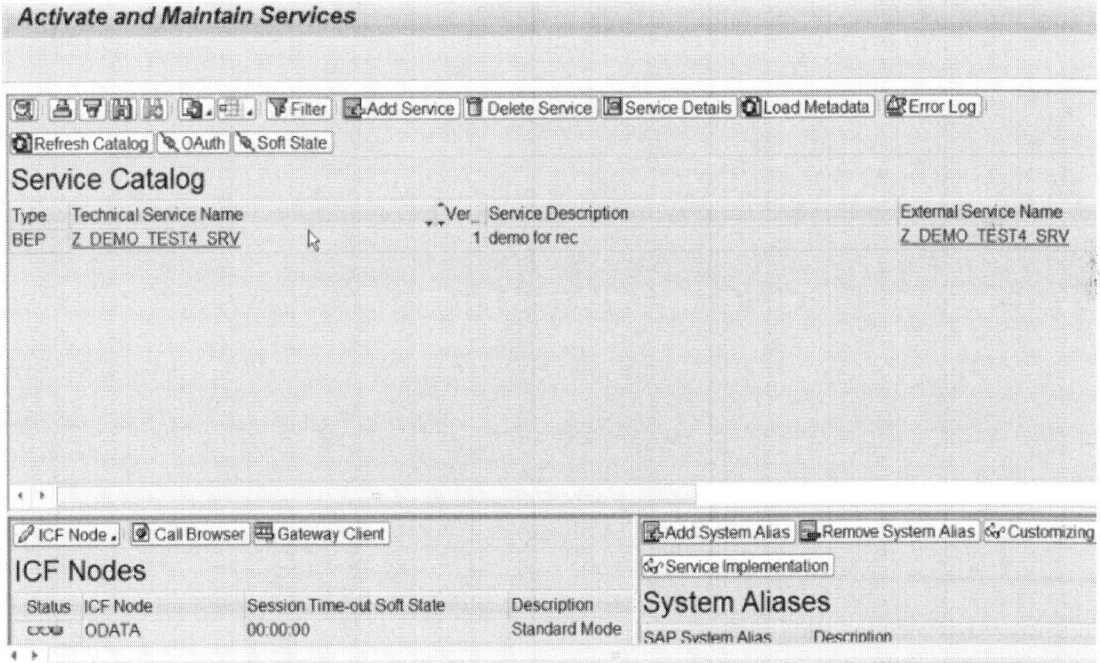

You can go to your Gateway client, some it is also referred to as a local browser inside SAP, to test your services.

Press Execute. It gives you some result, and the status code is 200, which means everything is okay.

35

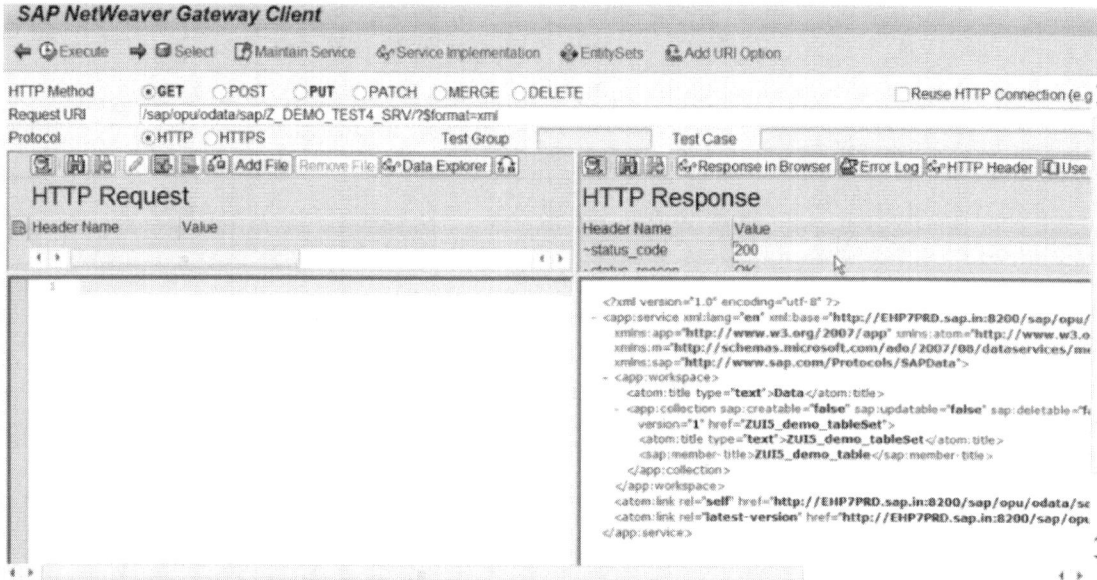

Now, we have successfully registered the services, so let's start implementing the CRUD operations.

Let's go back to the service builder which is the SEGW transaction. We are going to implement all the CRUD operations one by one.

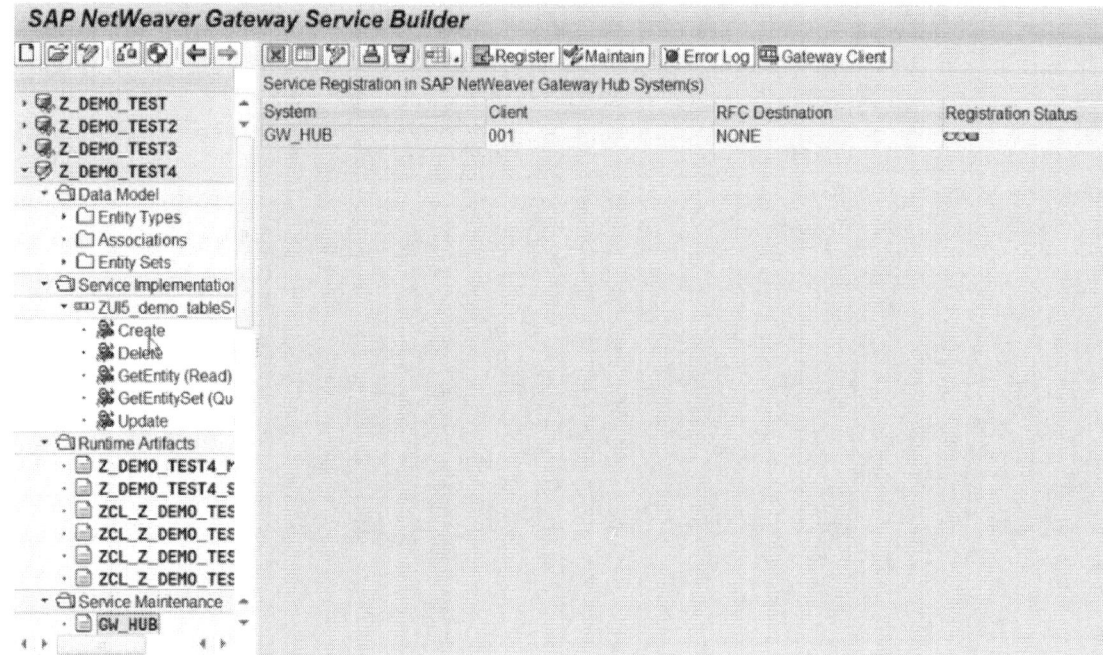

2.2 Query operation

The first operation which we will be implementing is Query, because it is like the SELECT * and is the most simple one. Right-click here, and Go to ABAP Workbench. As it says it has not yet been implemented, click on the check button to implement.

C:Create   R:Read   U:Update   D:Delete   **Q:Query**

GET

You can see that it opened an SE80 transaction, or the Object Viewer. You can go inside Methods, and inside Inherited Methods. There are 5 methods which we will be implemented.

> T-Code: se80
>
> This T-Code will be used for the purpose of find any object irrespective of the object type, it involves groups where you can search and navigate any particular object you like.

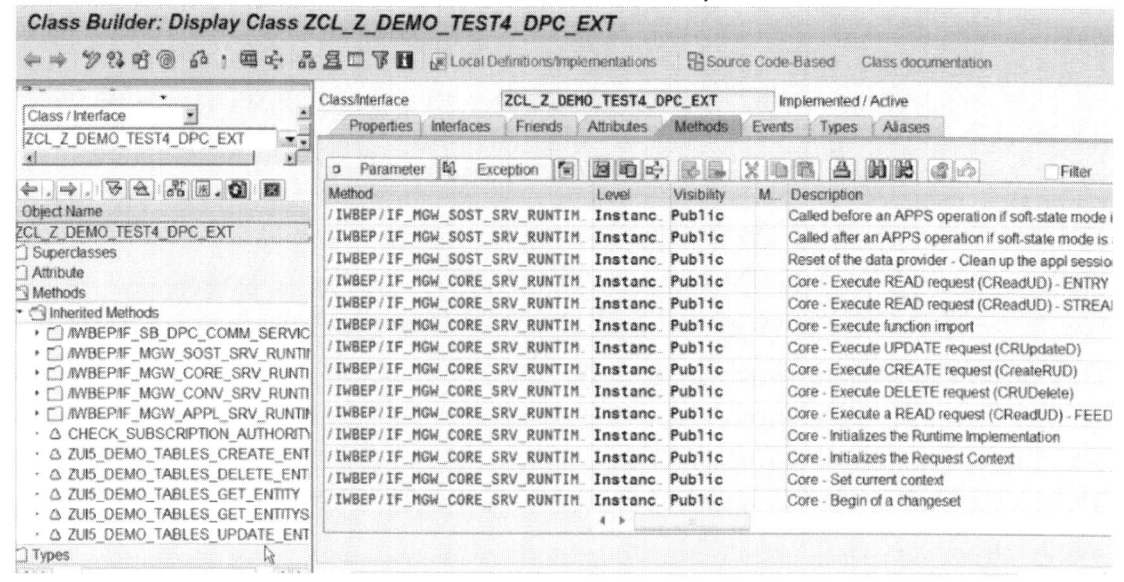

The first method which we would like to implement is *GET_ENTITYSET*. Just to give you an overview about this query, this is for selecting multiple columns like your SELECT *.

We have to implement the function *ZUI5_DEMO_TABLES_GET_ENTITYSET*, in which the first part of the name is the structure we gave while importing the Z structure from ABAP, and GET_ENTITYSET is the method which we are going to implement.

Right-click on the *GET_ENTITYSET*, and Redefine. It will open the method which we have to implement. Delete all the commented section there.

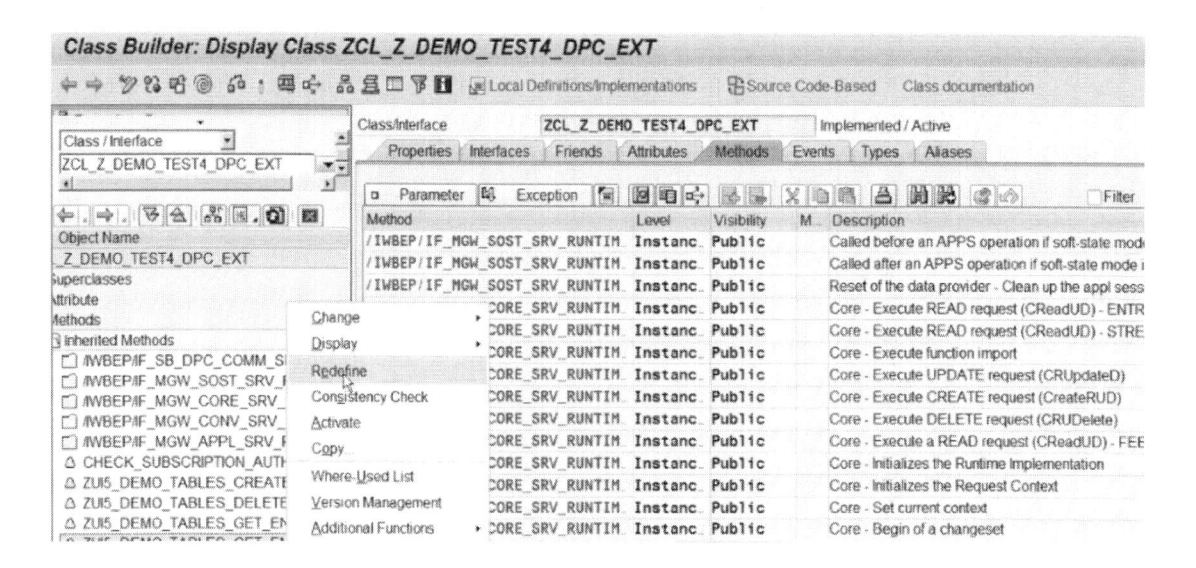

One thing you can see is that there are so many parameters here, some of which are import parameters to this method, and some are export parameters.

You can see ET_ENTITYSET, and also some exceptions which can be passed if some error occurred in your program.

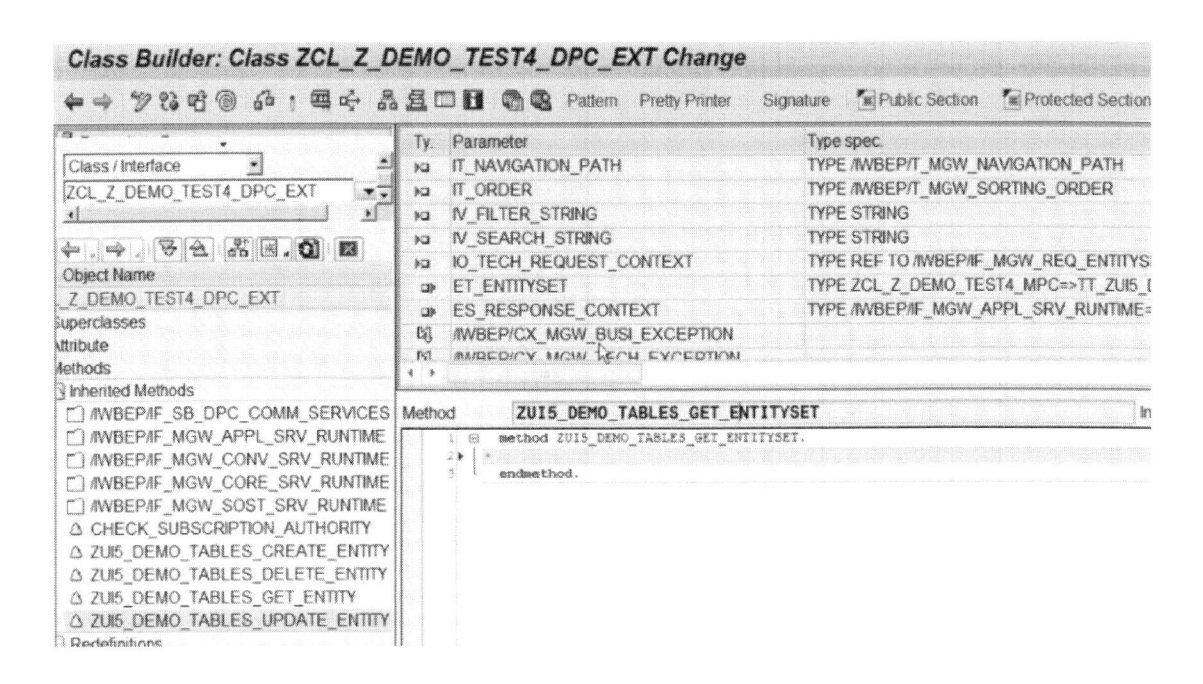

So the ABAP code for the query operation will be:

```
SELECT * on the ZUI5_DEMO_TABLE intoCORRESPONDING FIELDS OF
TABLE ET_ENTITYSET.
```

ET_ENTITYSET is our export parameter. It is actually the structure of this table. This is because we had created this service and imported the table structure; therefore the exporting table structure will be similar to that table.

We are just selecting the entire data of this table, and passing it to *ET_ENTITYSET*.

[Screenshot: Class Builder: Class ZCL_Z_DEMO_TEST4_DPC_EXT Change, showing method ZUI5_DEMO_TABLES_GET_ENTITYSET with code:
```
method ZUI5_DEMO_TABLES_GET_ENTITYSET.
SELECT * FROM ZUI5_DEMO_TABLE into CORRESPONDING FIELDS OF TABLE ET_ENTITYSET.
endmethod.
```
]

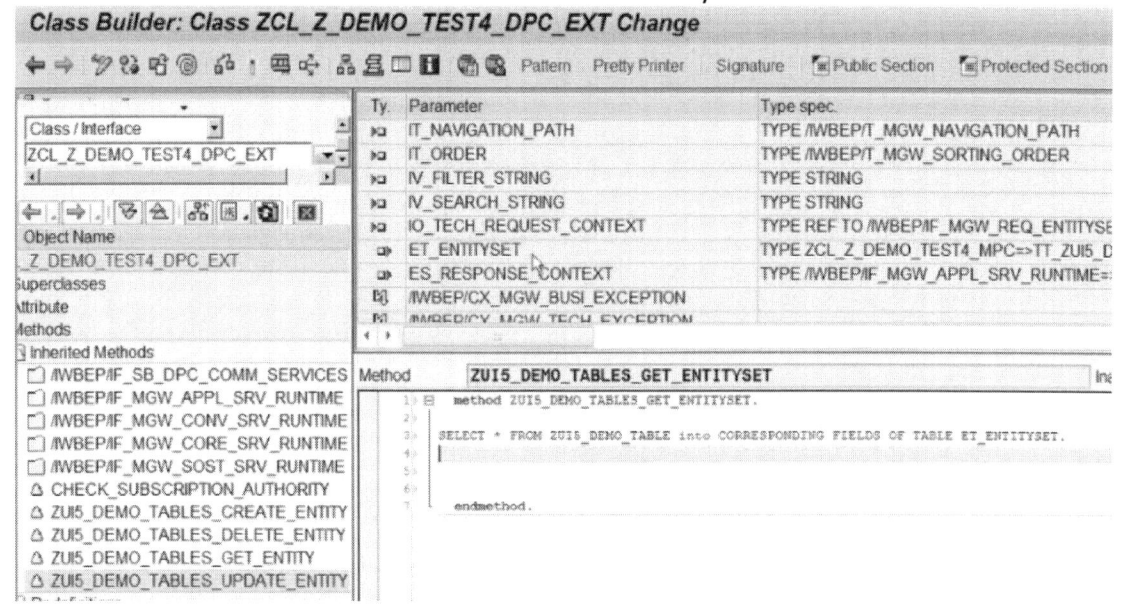

Save it, and activate *GET_ENTITYSET*. It selects some of the other objects which are dependent upon our *GET_ENTITYSET*. Press Continue and activate the object.

So how can we test this GET_ENTITYSET? Go to Gateway Client, and use this URL:

`/sap/opu/odata/sap/Z_DEMO_TEST4_SRV/ZUI5_demo_tableSet/?$format=json`

Z_DEMO_TEST4_SRV is the name of our service, ZUI5_demo_tableSet is how it recognizes the name of the method and *?$format=json* is the additional functionality which specifies what output format you want to see.

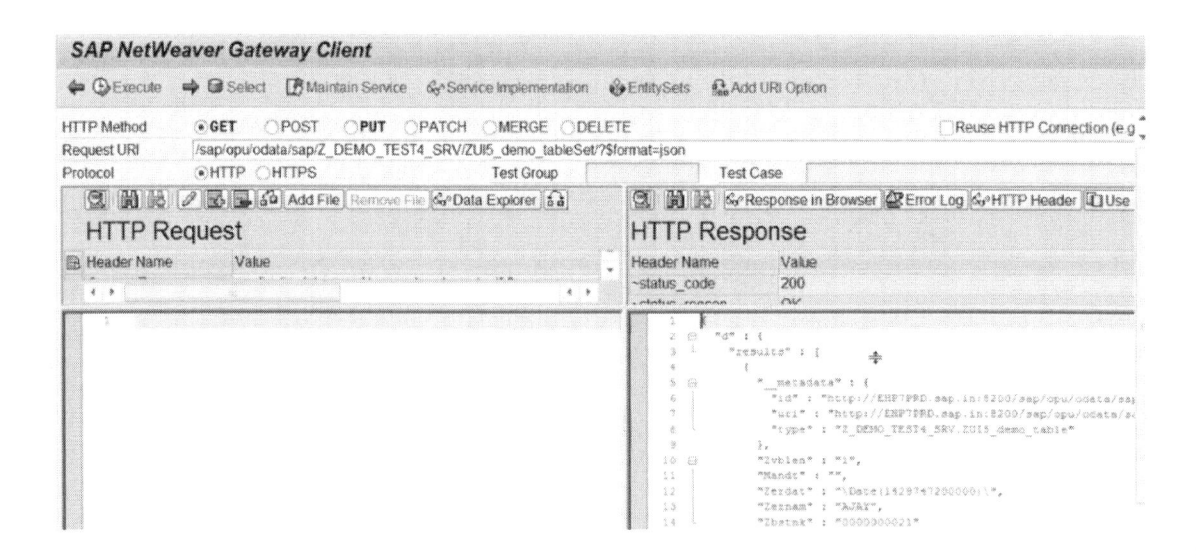

[Screenshot: SAP NetWeaver Gateway Client showing HTTP GET request with Request URI /sap/opu/odata/sap/Z_DEMO_TEST4_SRV/ZUI5_demo_tableSet/?$format=json, HTTP Response status_code 200, and JSON response containing results with metadata, Zvblen, Mandt, Zerdat, Zeinam, Zbstnk fields.]

The HTTP method should be GET because we are reading the information. If you press Execute, then you can see that all records of the table are given to us. You can see that there are 4 records in the table, and are shown here in the gateway client as well.

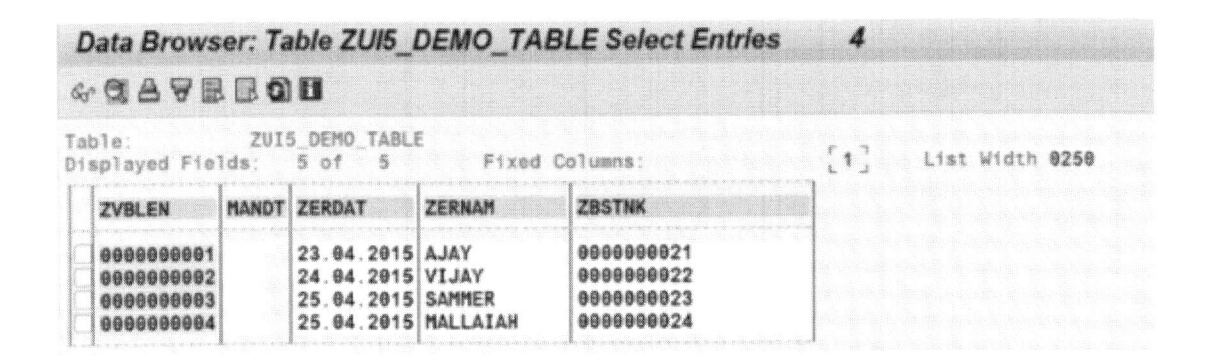

```
Data Browser: Table ZUI5_DEMO_TABLE Select Entries    4

Table:           ZUI5_DEMO_TABLE
Displayed Fields:   5 of   5      Fixed Columns:        [1]    List Width 0250

ZVBLEN     MANDT  ZERDAT      ZERNAM    ZBSTNK
0000000001        23.04.2015  AJAY      0000000021
0000000002        24.04.2015  VIJAY     0000000022
0000000003        25.04.2015  SAMMER    0000000023
0000000004        25.04.2015  MALLAIAH  0000000024
```

The same thing can be done in your web browser. You have to add the host name and the port number, and the rest is the same as what you write in your Gateway client. When we enter, we get the same results.

```
{
  - d: {
    - results: [
      - {
        - __metadata: {
            id: "http://ehp7prd.sap.in:8200/sap/opu/odata/sap/Z_DEMO_TEST4_SRV/ZUI5_demo_tableSet('1')",
            uri: "http://ehp7prd.sap.in:8200/sap/opu/odata/sap/Z_DEMO_TEST4_SRV/ZUI5_demo_tableSet('1')",
            type: "Z_DEMO_TEST4_SRV.ZUI5_demo_table"
          },
          Zvblen: "1",
          Mandt: "",
          Zerdat: "/Date(1429747200000)/",
          Zernam: "AJAY",
          Zbstnk: "0000000021"
      },
      - {
        - __metadata: {
            id: "http://ehp7prd.sap.in:8200/sap/opu/odata/sap/Z_DEMO_TEST4_SRV/ZUI5_demo_tableSet('2')",
            uri: "http://ehp7prd.sap.in:8200/sap/opu/odata/sap/Z_DEMO_TEST4_SRV/ZUI5_demo_tableSet('2')",
            type: "Z_DEMO_TEST4_SRV.ZUI5_demo_table"
          },
          Zvblen: "2",
          Mandt: "",
          Zerdat: "/Date(1429833600000)/",
          Zernam: "VIJAY",
          Zbstnk: "0000000022"
      },
      - {
        - __metadata: {
            id: "http://ehp7prd.sap.in:8200/sap/opu/odata/sap/Z_DEMO_TEST4_SRV/ZUI5_demo_tableSet('3')",
            uri: "http://ehp7prd.sap.in:8200/sap/opu/odata/sap/Z_DEMO_TEST4_SRV/ZUI5_demo_tableSet('3')",
            type: "Z_DEMO_TEST4_SRV.ZUI5_demo_table"
```

Gateway client testing should be done first before the browser testing.

This is the implementation of your Query, which is like your SELECT * or selecting multiple columns.

The next thing which we are going to see is the Read operation, which will be like SELECT single.

2.3 Read operation

C:Create R:Read U:Update D:Delete Q:Query

GET

For example, you have this table and you want to read this column which has the key value of 2. To do that, we have to implement GET_ENTITY. Previously, we implemented GET_ENTITYSET to read multiple or all records.

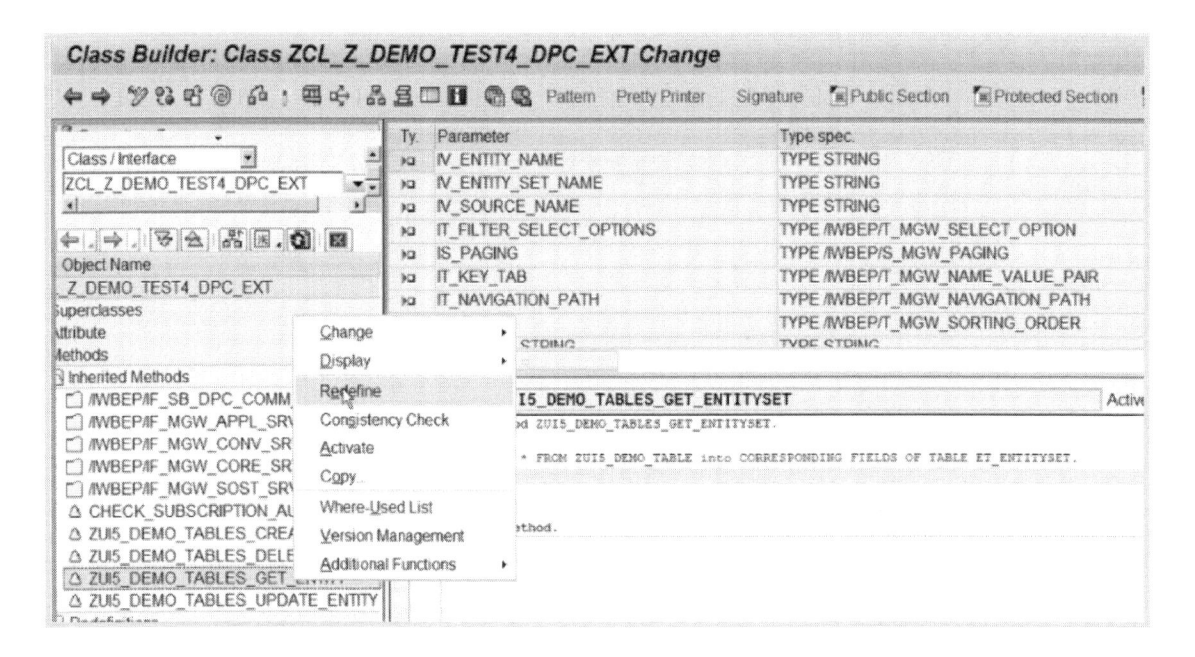

We go to Class Builder, right-click on GET_ENTITY, and Redefine. Remove the commented section.

This is the test sample ABAP code:

```
DATA:lv_vbeln TYPE vbak-vbeln,
ls_key_tab TYPE /iwbep/s_mgw_name_value_pair.
```

```
*Get the key property values
READ TABLE it_key_tab INTO ls_key_tab WITH KEY name =
'Zvblen' .
"lv_vbeln = ls_key_tab-value.
SELECT single
"ZVBELN MANDT ZERDAT ZERNAM ZBSTNK
* from ZUI5_demo_table into
CORRESPONDING FIELDS OF er_entity where zvblen eq
ls_key_tab-value .
if sy-subrc <>0."Throw exception here
ENDIF.
```

We are going to use some of the importing parameters here because the key values will determine which column to read from this table.

For example, if we want to read the second record, then we should be passing this value so that we can filter this table with this value.

This particular value will be passed via our URL and that URL value will be available to us in our methods by our importing parameters. These importing parameters, specifically the IT_KEY_TAB, will be having all of our key values that are passed via URL.

/sap/opu/odata/sap/Z_DEMO_TEST4_SRV/ZUI5_demo_tableSet('0000000002')

We're going to READ TABLE it_key_tab WITH KEY name = 'Zvblen' (which is the key field of the structure), so we can read this name.

Once we get the value which is passed via URL, then we can easily write a SELECT single * from ZUI5_demo_table (the table) into CORRESPONDING FIELDS OF er_entity (which is exported from this function) where zvblen eq ls_key_tab-value (which is what we got from our URL).

Save this code, activate, and put a debugging point.

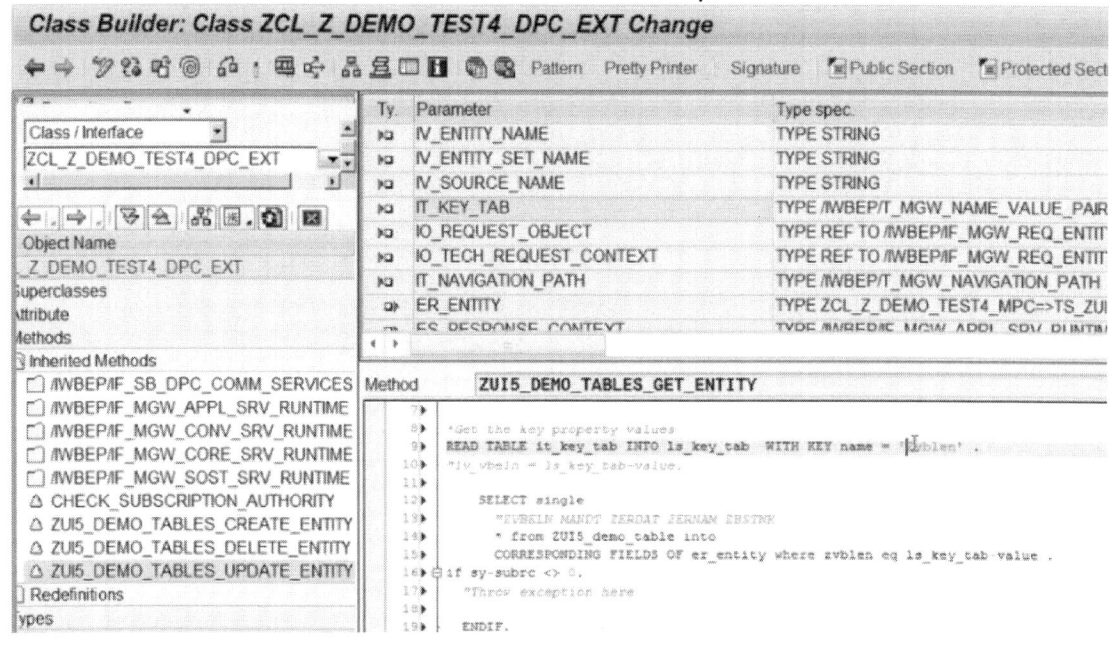

Go to the Gateway Client, and the URL to access the GET_ENTITY is:

```
/sap/opu/odata/sap/Z_DEMO_TEST4_SRV/ZUI5_demo_tableSet('0000000002')
```

Which is same as mentioned above.

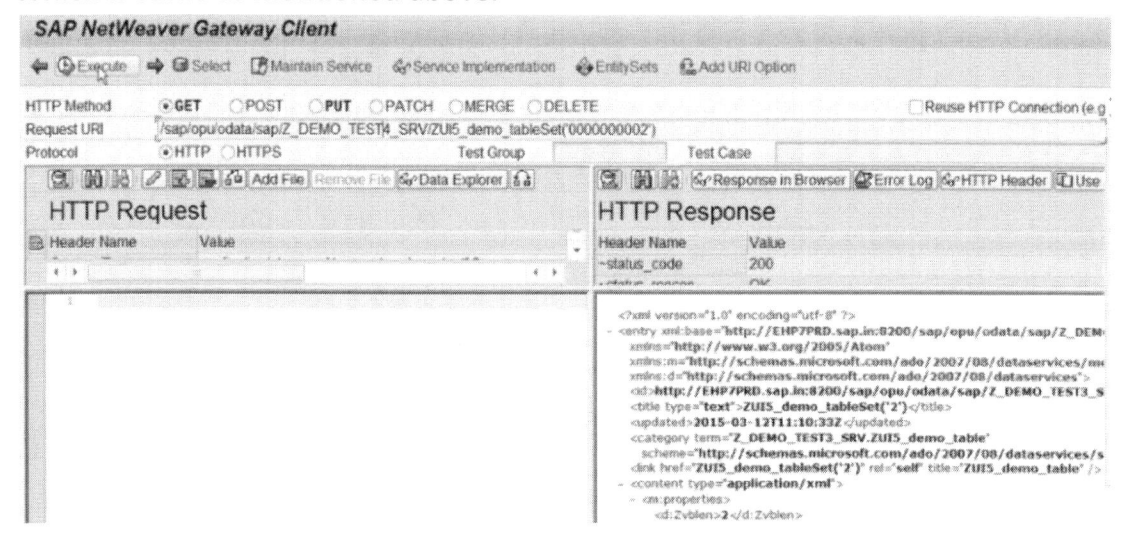

This is the same as with GET_ENTITYSET, but with additional key values in the bracket. If we execute, it will stop at the debugging point.

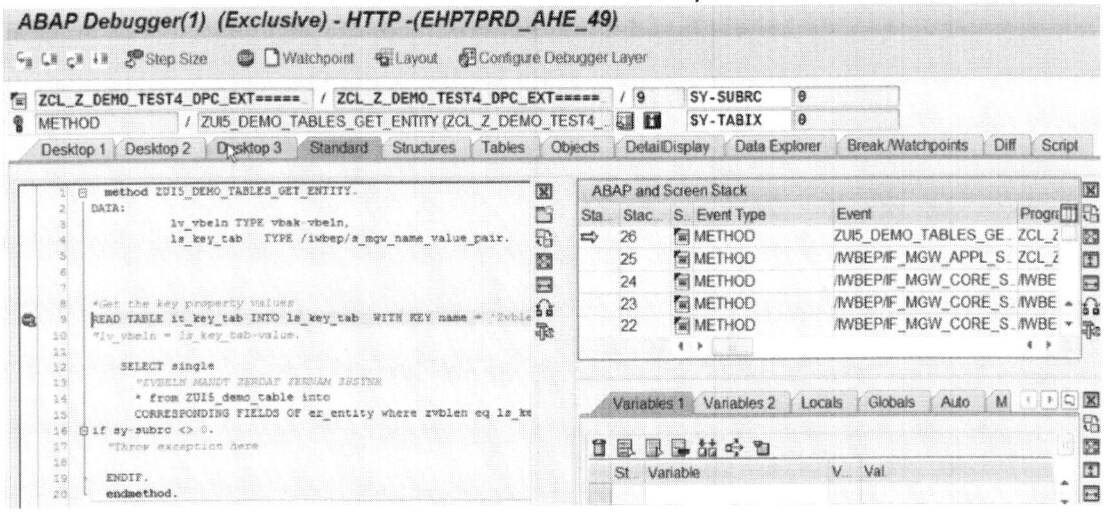

This IT_KEY_TAB is actually the import parameter. If we go inside it, we can see that it has only one value, and has 3 columns. Column 1 is Row, Column 2 is a CString value called NAME, and Column 3 is also a CString value called VALUE.

Zvblen is the key of the table and the value which we passed via URL is the 0000000002, and we are just reading that particular record into ls_key_tab.

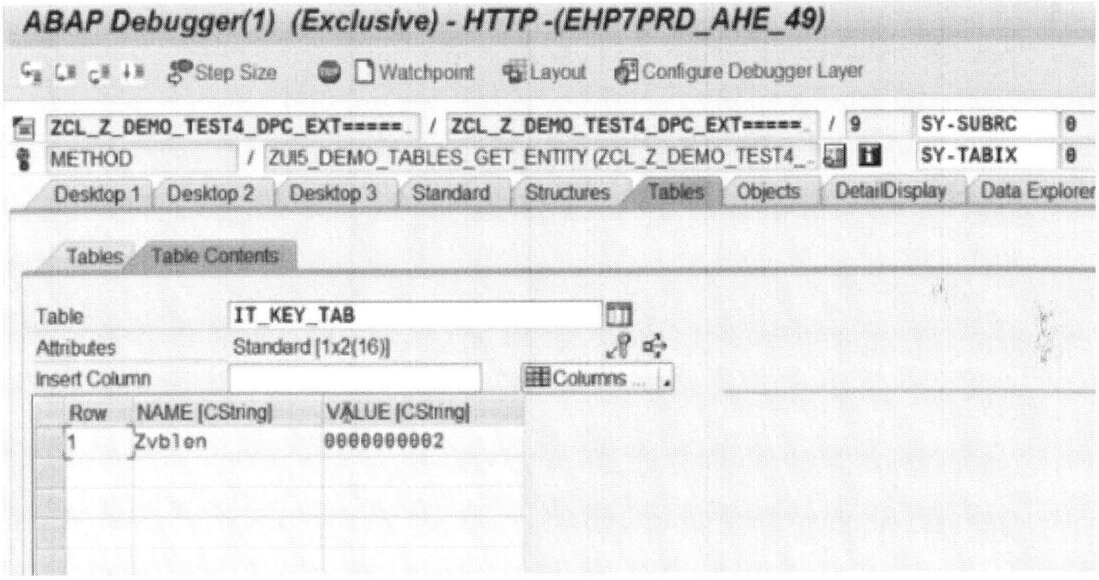

IT_KEY_TAB is a table basically from the structure : /wbep/s_mgw_name_value_pair.

Inside our methods, we're using this structure so that we can have a local variable that has the same structure of this table.

Where we can store our records is available in IT_KEY_TAB, and we can pass it to our SELECT single query. Here, you can see this local variable we're accessing the variable ls_key_tab-value.

Going back to our ABAP debugger, the value of the lead operation if we put the debugging point here should be *0000000002*.

After the operation, the sy-subrc value will be zero. If it is not zero, then you can throw an exception here, which will be reflected in your service, and the message will be shown. If it is successful, then it will just populate our er_entity table.

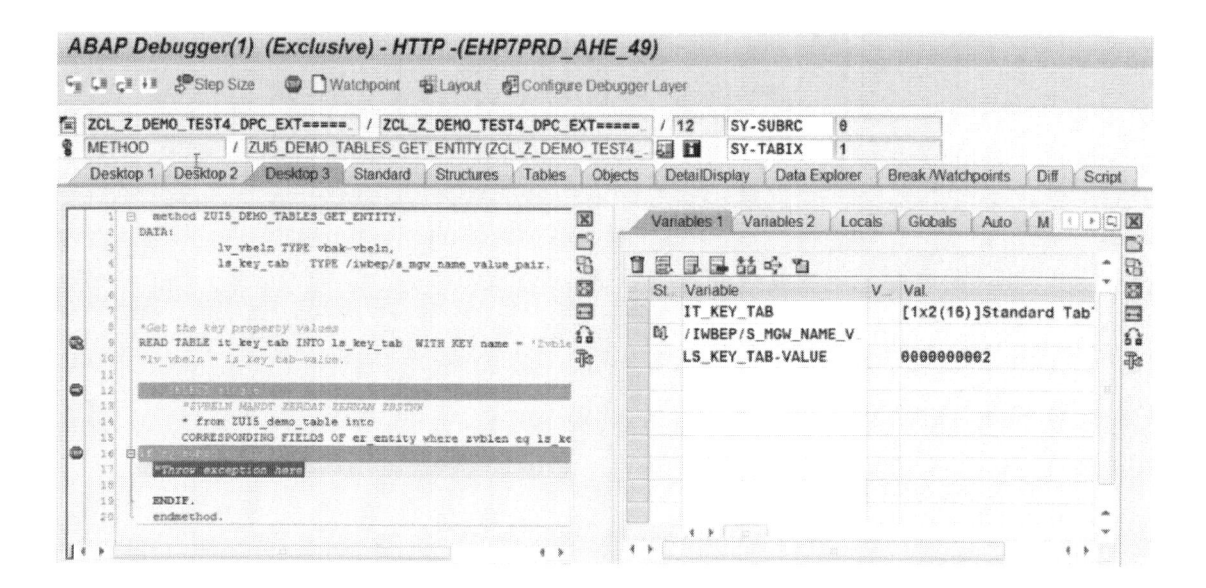

First of all, let us see sy-subrc, it should be zero. Double-click on er_entity. The value inside er_entity will be the single record which was read, and which is the same second record as presented in ourse11. This is what will be exported.

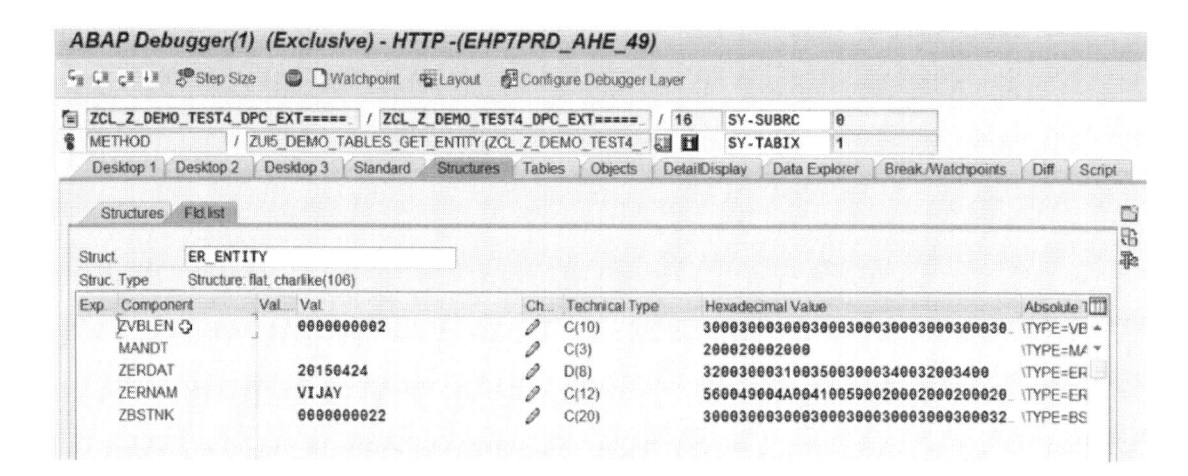

Just to give you a heads up, we implemented this READ operation. The URL which is required is this one:

```
/sap/opu/odata/sap/Z_DEMO_TEST4_SRV/ZUI5_demo_tableSet('0000000002')
```

Because it is like a single selection, you should pass a key to your selection so that a single record can be read. You can have multiple keys as well, separated by a comma, so that your ls_key_tab will have multiple records.

This is how simple it is to implement your Read operation. In the next section, we will create part of the CRUDQ operation.

2.4 Create operation

C:Create R:Read U:Update D:Delete Q:Query
POST

Create is used to create new records in your table, and the POST operation of your HTTP AJAX request is used here. The Create process is a bit tricky to run or use, but the implementation is quite simple.

So let's go to our SAP screen and see how to implement the Create operation.

To implement it, we will go back to the Class Builder screen for our project. We can see the CREATE_ENTITYSET here in the methods. Right-click, and select Redefine. You can see the method we have to implement. Delete the commented code. Copy this code here.

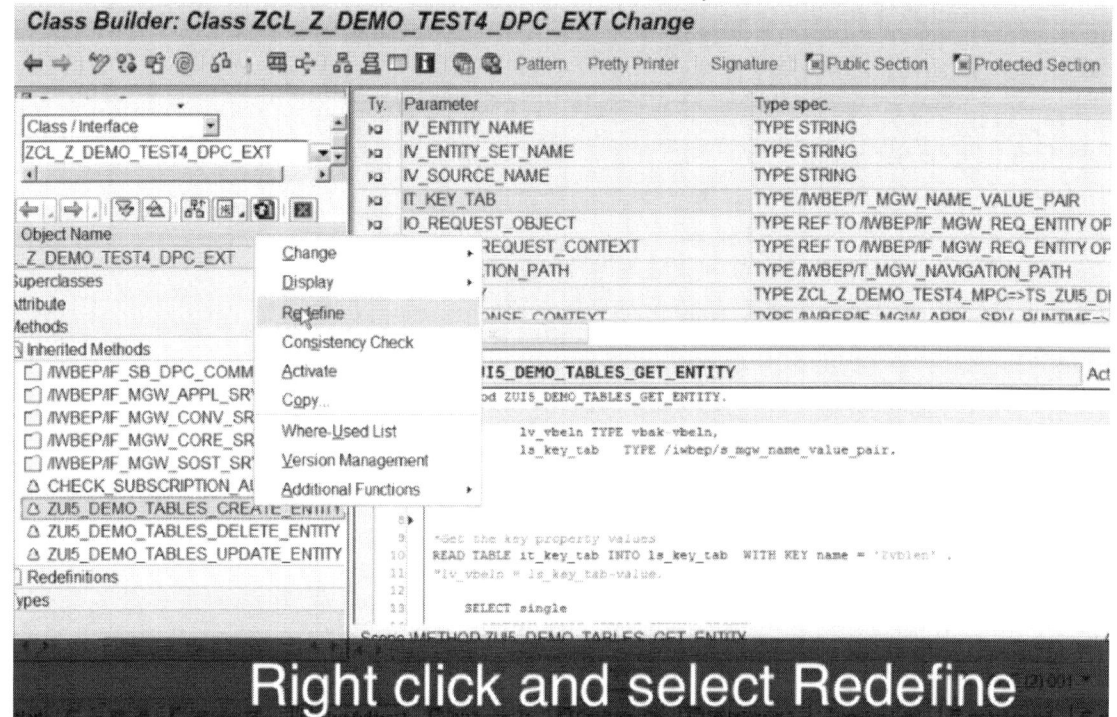

Let's analyze the ABAP code below:

```
DATA: ls_request_input_data TYPE
ZCL_Z_DEMO_TEST3_MPC=>TS_ZUI5_DEMO_TABLE,ls_userinfo TYPE
ZUI5_DEMO_TABLE.
```

* Read Request Data

```
io_data_provider->read_entry_data( IMPORTING es_data =
ls_request_input_data ).
```

* Fill workarea to be inserted

```
ls_userinfo-ZVBLEN = ls_request_input_data-ZVBLEN.
```

" ls_userinfo-MANDAT = .

```
ls_userinfo-ZERDAT = ls_request_input_data-ZERDAT.ls_userinfo-
ZERNAM = ls_request_input_data-ZERNAM.ls_userinfo-ZBSTNK =
ls_request_input_data-ZBSTNK.
```

* Insert Data in table ZUSERINFO

```
INSERT ZUI5_DEMO_TABLE FROM ls_userinfo.IF sy-subrc = 0.
er_entity = ls_request_input_data.
```
"Fill Exporting parameter ER_ENTITY
```
ENDIF.
```

What this code does is actually reading is an IO_DATA_PROVIDER.

What basically happens when you are sending some data to create a new record is that that data will be available in IO_DATA_PROVIDER. This is actually a table you have to read and you will import the values into this particular work area: ls_request_input_data.

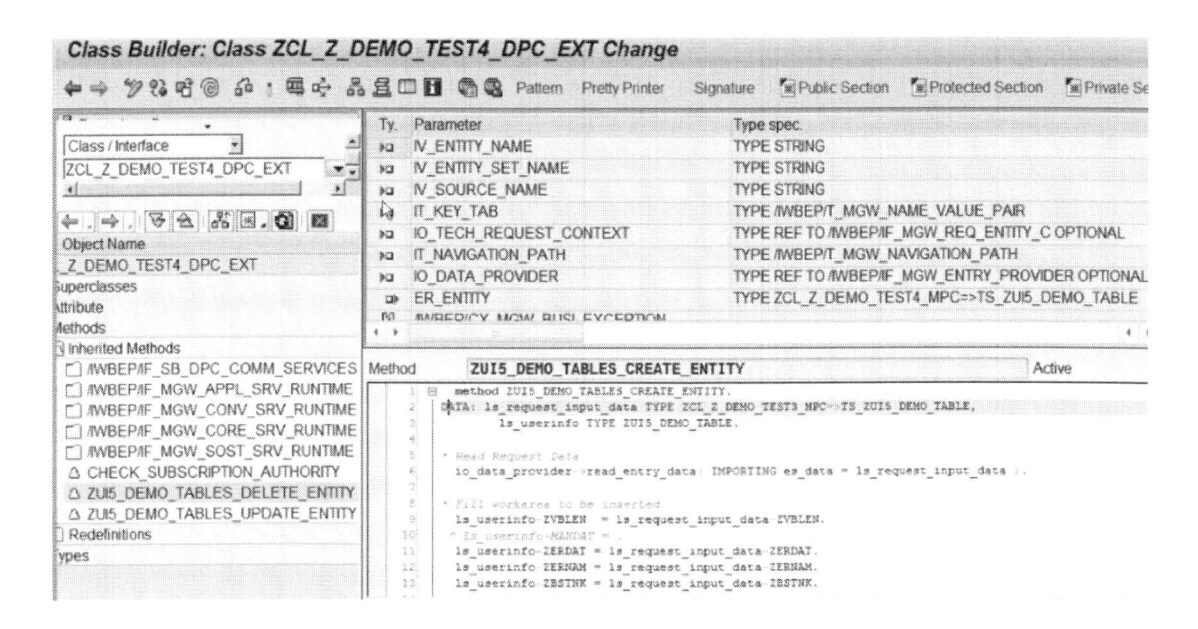

Once we get the values, we directly call the INSERT statement and use the ls_userinfo. ls_userinfo is a structure, and we are individually copying all of our past data from ls_request_input_data into ls_userinfo.

We are also putting all of the data back to er_entity, which is the variable which is exported out of this method.

Let's now run this method using our gateway client.

If you go to Gateway client, you first have to get the data. To get the data of one particular record or row, you have to use GET_ENTITY which we created in the previous section, and Execute.

Now we will copy this response, by clicking *Use As Request(as shown in below image)*. Once we do that, you see in the left side that you got some data there, and the content type was copied as well.

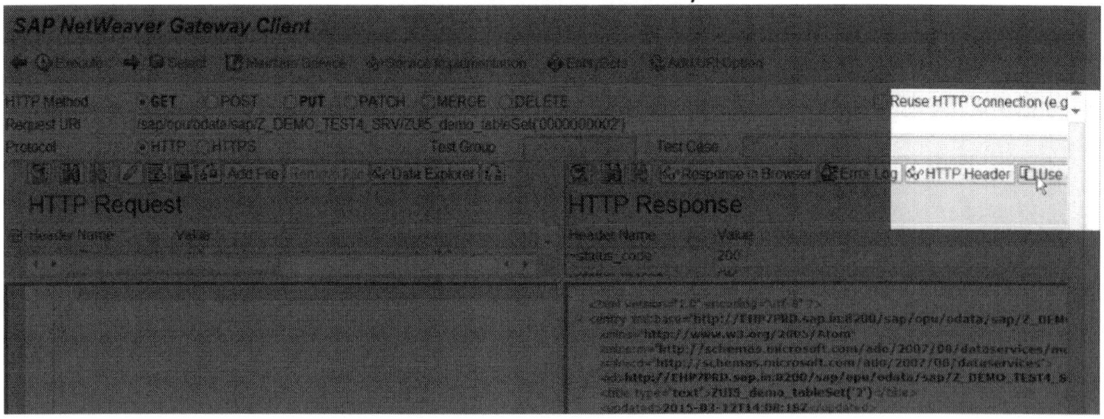

Now let's proceed to create a new record.

What we have to use to create a new record is POST. Your Create methods will be automatically executed.

T-Code: /IWFND/ERROR_LOG

The Error Log for SAP NetWeaver Gateway hub systems is a helpful addition to the existing Application Log Viewer and provides detailed context information about errors that have occurred at runtime.

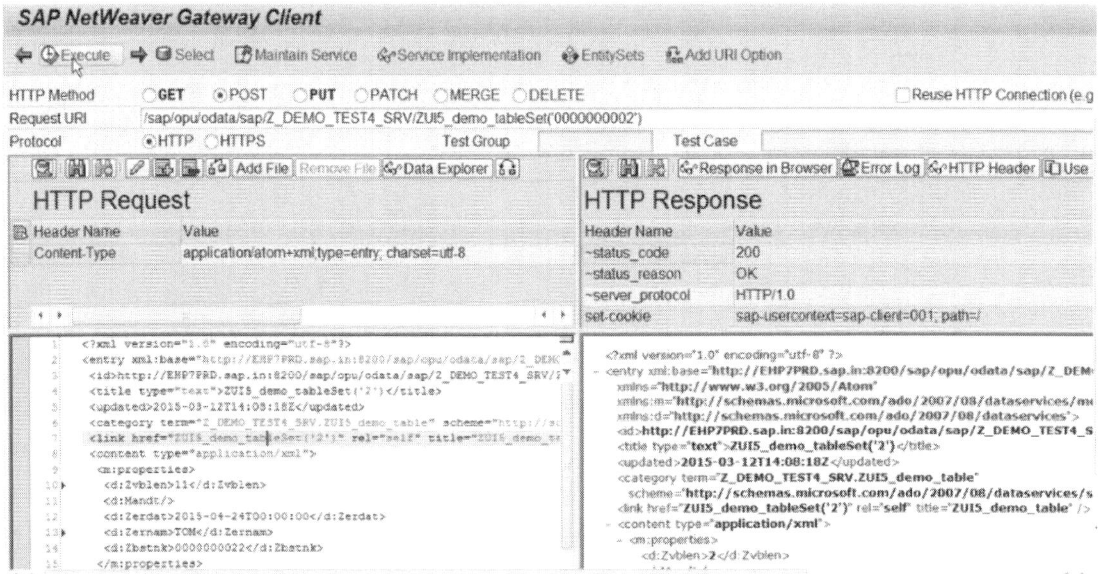

But while performing the operation you can see there are some errors, and it says "Method Not Allowed". Let us go to this error transaction: /IWFND/ERROR_LOG.

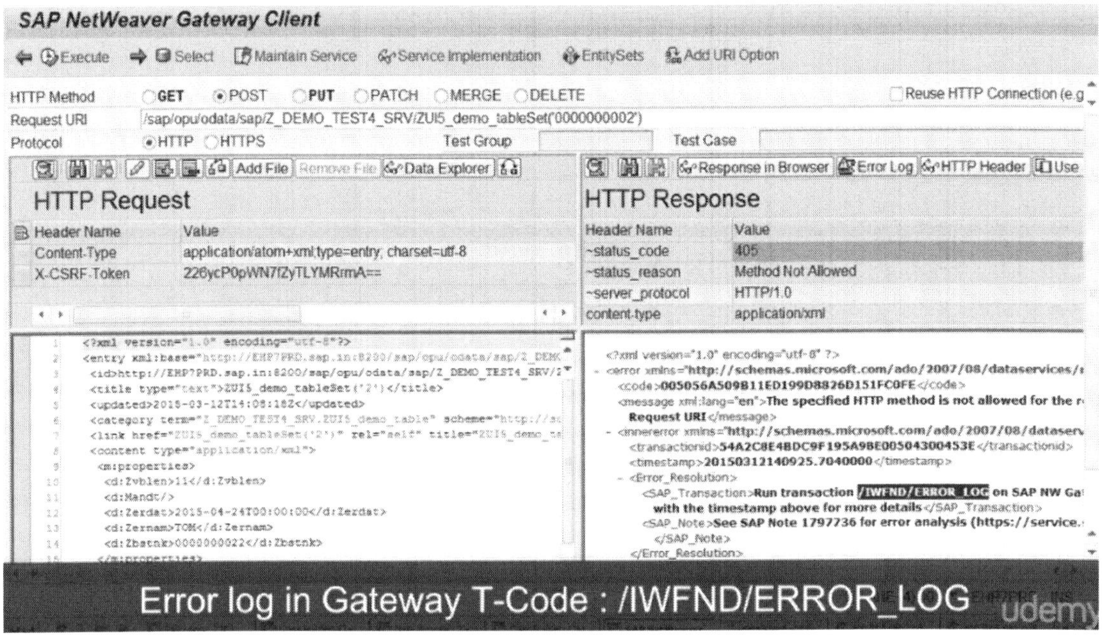
SAP NetWeaver Gateway Client
HTTP Request
HTTP Response
Error log in Gateway T-Code : /IWFND/ERROR_LOG

This is for checking errors. When you are doing some developments in Gateway, it is frequent that you get errors.

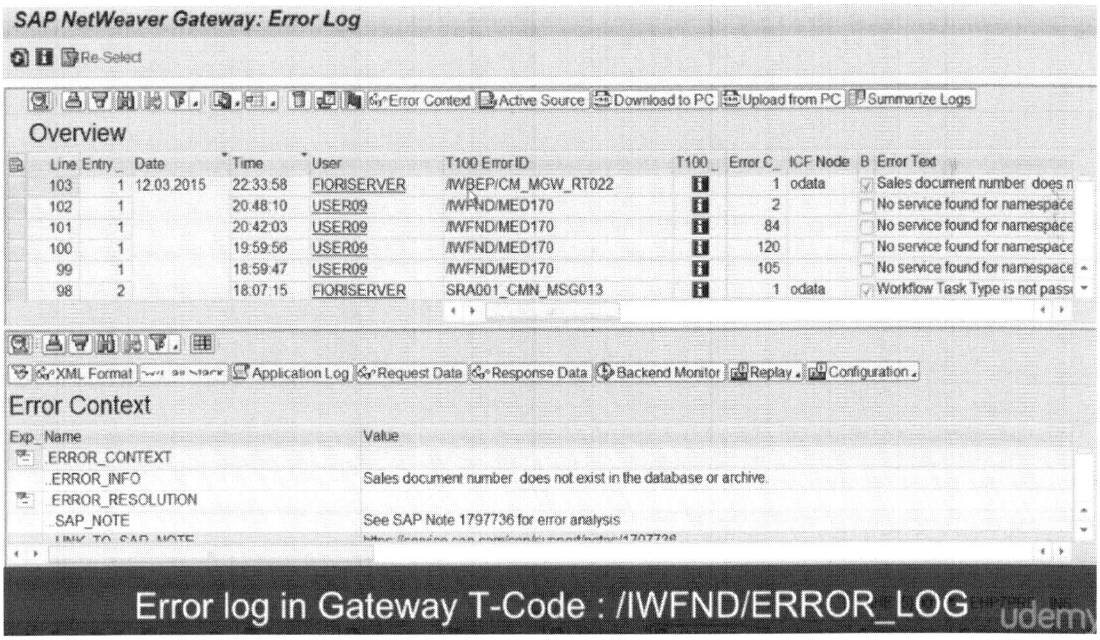
SAP NetWeaver Gateway: Error Log
Overview
Error Context
Error log in Gateway T-Code : /IWFND/ERROR_LOG

It says that the data we provided does not exist in the archive. I'm passing this as my parameter, and I don't require this parameter. Get rid of it, and try to execute again.

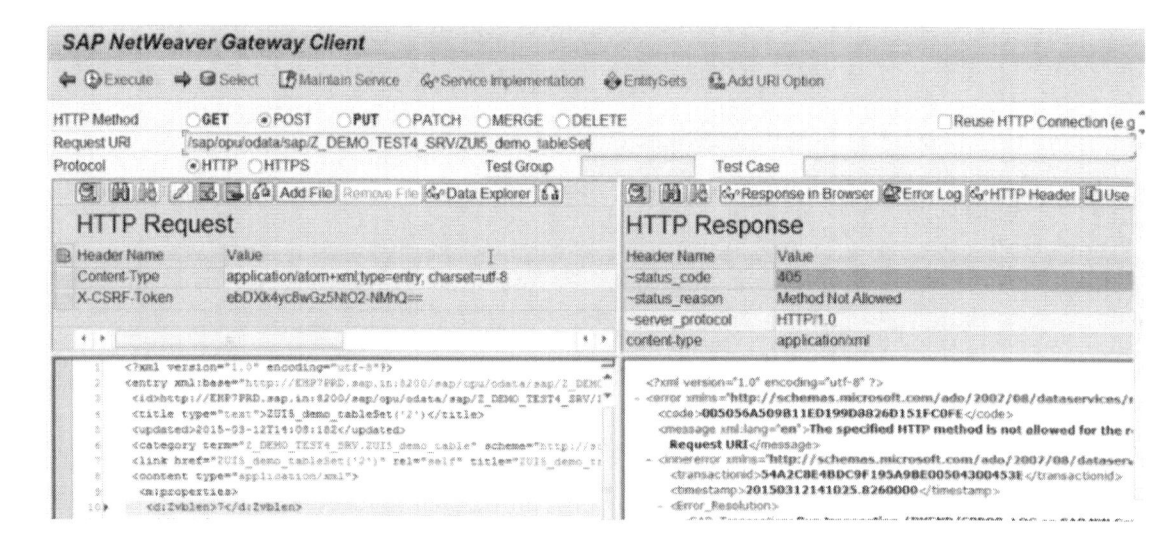

/sap/opu/odata/sap/Z_DEMO_TEST4_SRV/ZUI5_demo_tableSet

The problem was created by our parameter here, because when you do a Create call then the data should be passed in your response.

The URL should be ZUI5_demo_tableset which is the GET_ENTITYSET URL. You don't have to specify in the key which records you're going to update, because this is not an Update statement, but a Create statement. We have to give a generic URL, and that URL should be off-set type.

You can see that in our Redefinitions path, we have our Create function there to run this method with that data which we have passed in the response body, and we will give the data to the set URL.

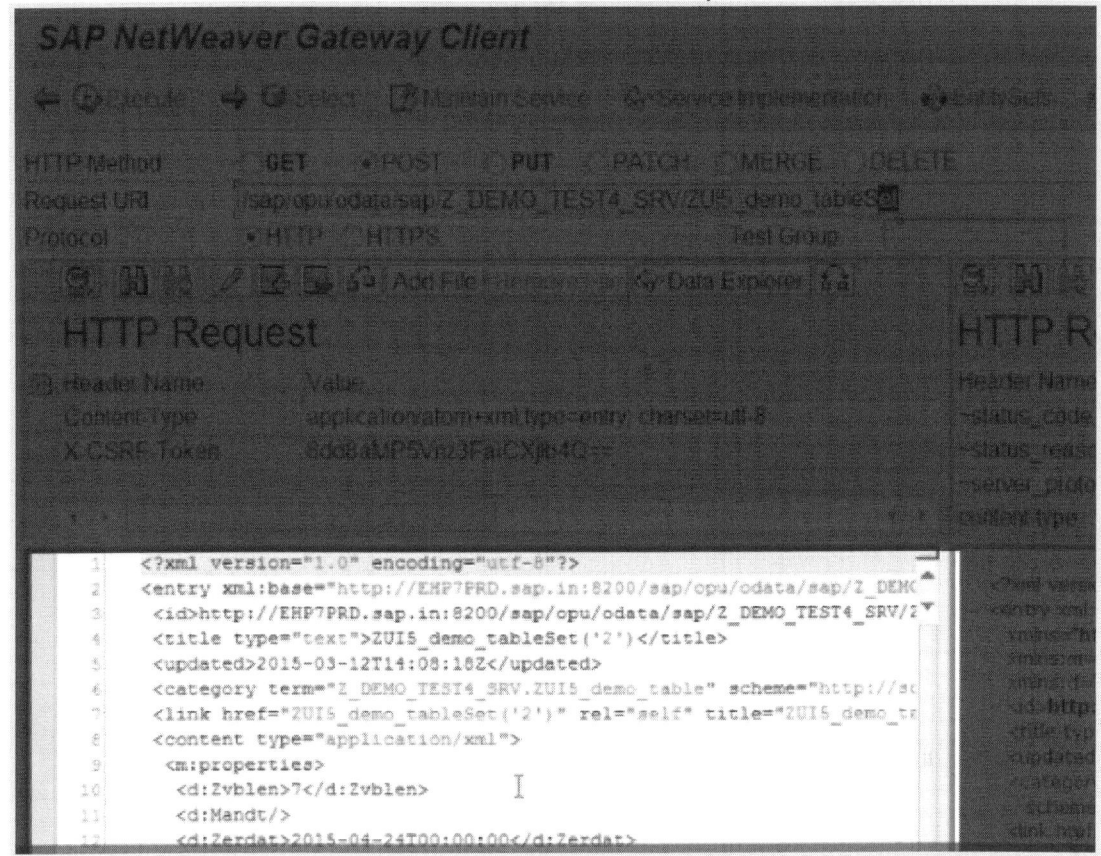

One of the important things when we do an AJAX call via UI5 application is that you also have to give the X-CSRF-Token. X-CSRF-Token is automatically copied in the response when the data is used as request, but when you are calling from the UI5 application; you have to manually give the X-CSRF-Token.

It is used to prevent forgeries. This is a security mechanism so that the web service only accepts data from legitimate sources that already have X-CSRF-Token previously.

When you do a GET call, you automatically get an X-CSRF-Token, which could be used via POST request as well.

SAP® Netweaver Gateway

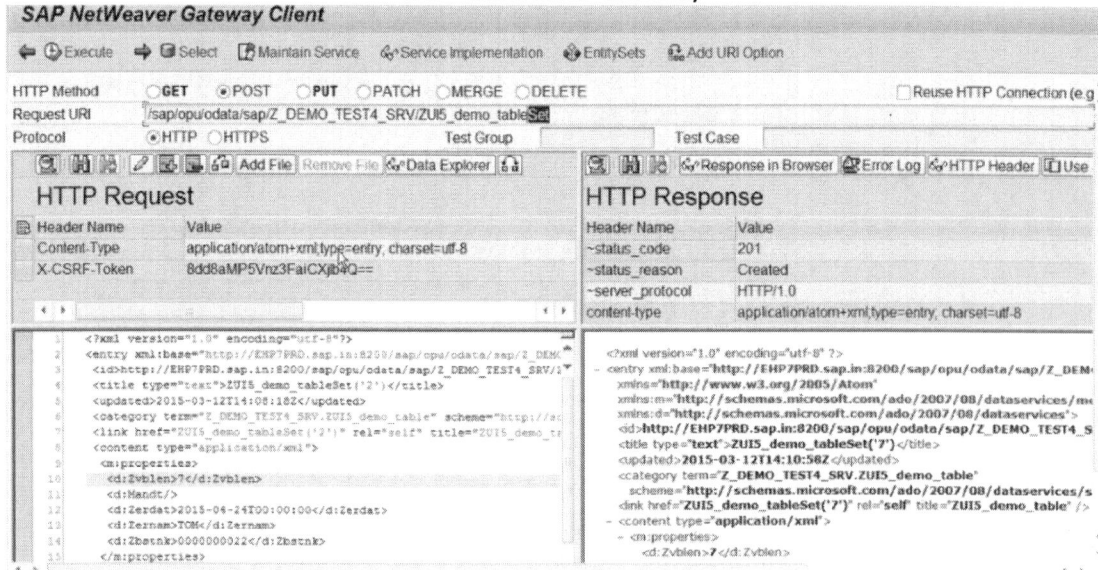

[Screenshot of SAP NetWeaver Gateway Client showing HTTP Request and HTTP Response panels with XML content for a PUT operation on ZUI5_demo_tableSet]

If we are doing this with a web browser, to do a GET request for the first time, the Gateway will ask for credentials so the security is maintained via service calls.

Now, let's go to the second functionality which is our Update scenario.

2.5 Update operation

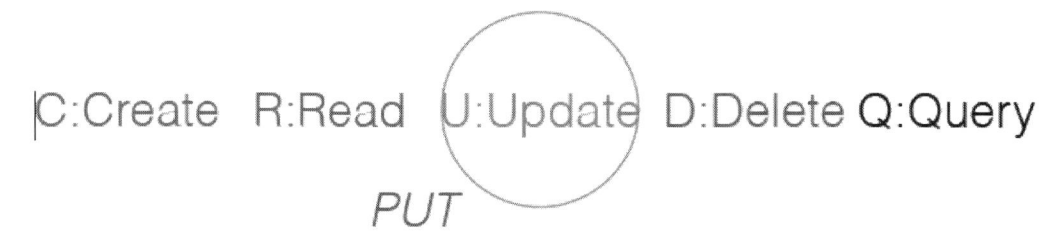

C:Create R:Read U:Update D:Delete Q:Query

PUT

We go to our Update scenario. Here, we will read the data entry and will use the UPDATE ABAP statement. We will debug this program this time so that you can see what is happening inside your ABAP code.

Let us go to the Class Builder, and this time we are going to implement the Update functionality. Let's Redefine.

SAP® Netweaver Gateway

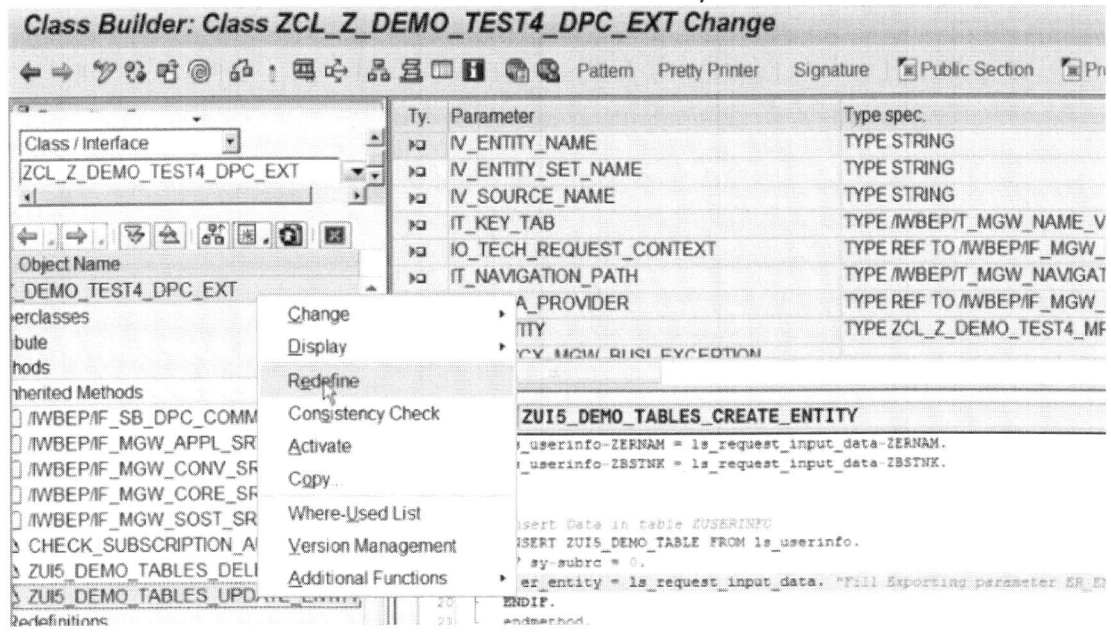

[Screenshot: Class Builder: Class ZCL_Z_DEMO_TEST4_DPC_EXT Change, with context menu showing Change, Display, Redefine, Consistency Check, Activate, Copy, Where-Used List, Version Management, Additional Functions]

Get rid of all the comments and coding, and copy and paste this new coding.

```
DATA: ls_request_input_data TYPE zcl_z_demo_test3_mpc=>ts_zui5_demo_table, ls_userinfo TYPE zui5_demo_table.
* Read Request Data
io_data_provider->read_entry_data( IMPORTING es_data = ls_request_input_data ).
" Update fields of table ZUSERINFO
UPDATE zui5_demo_tableSET
zvblen = ls_request_input_data-zvblen
zerdat = ls_request_input_data-zerdat
zernam = ls_request_input_data-zernam
zbstnk = ls_request_input_data-zbstnk
where zvblen = ls_request_input_data-zvblen.
IF sy-subrc= 0.
er_entity = ls_request_input_data.
ENDIF.
```

Save it, and then Activate. We have the active object generated.

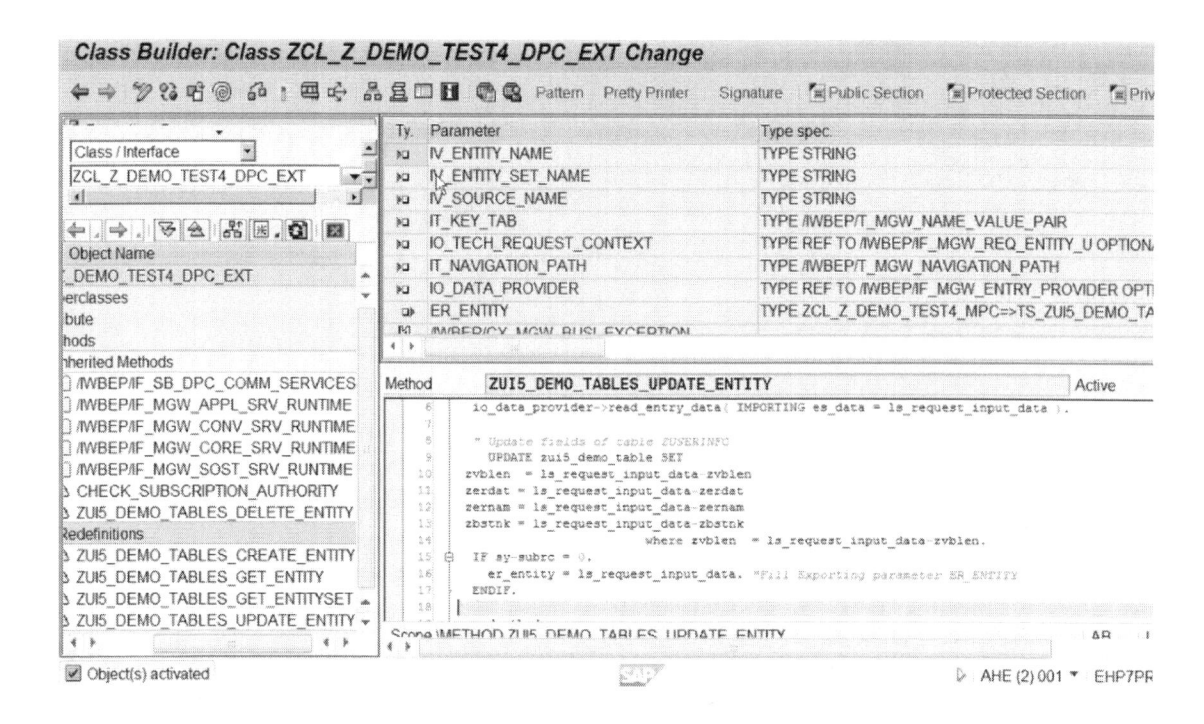

We can see that the "Tom" which we created as a new entry is now in our table.

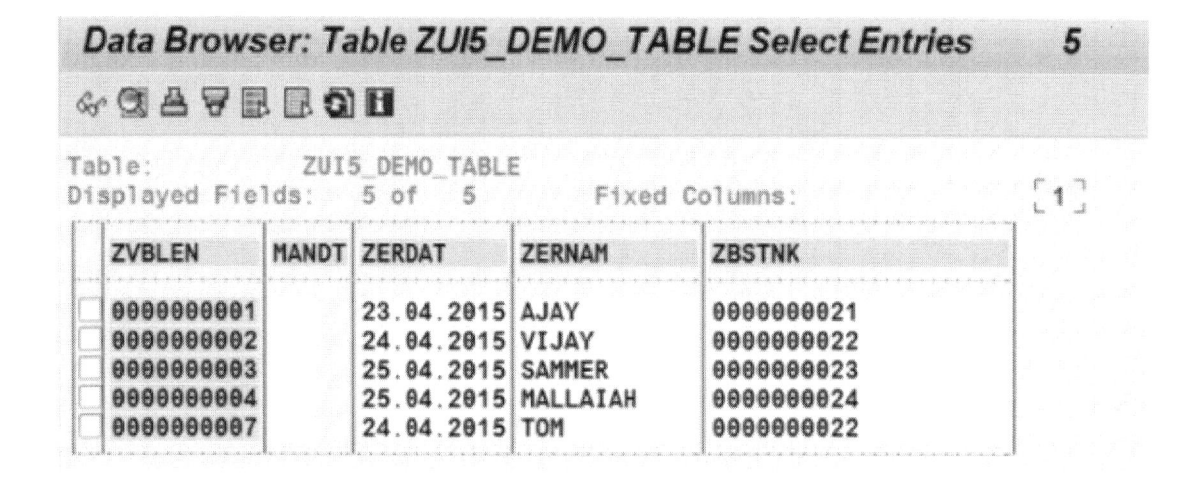

Now, with the Update record, we will update this created entry, and we will change the name of TOM to JERRY. To test your Call Update, you go to Gateway client.

What we have to do now is to read the record, because you have to know which records you want to update. First, you need to do a Read operation to get the records, so you can use that response as a request again.

`/sap/opu/odata/sap/Z_DEMO_TEST4_SRV/ZUI5_demo_tableSet('0000000007')`

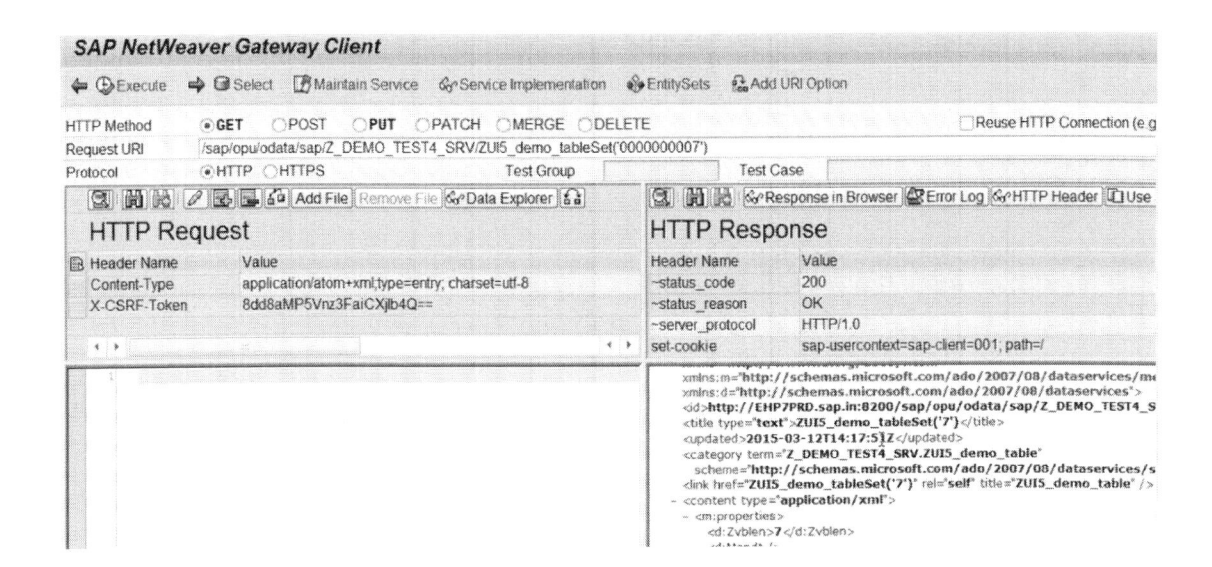

Do a GET request. We're getting the "Tom" data which we just created in the table. You can see the HTTP Response, and the data which is in XML is the response body. Click on *Use As Request*, to copy the same response as a request. This is copied in the left side.

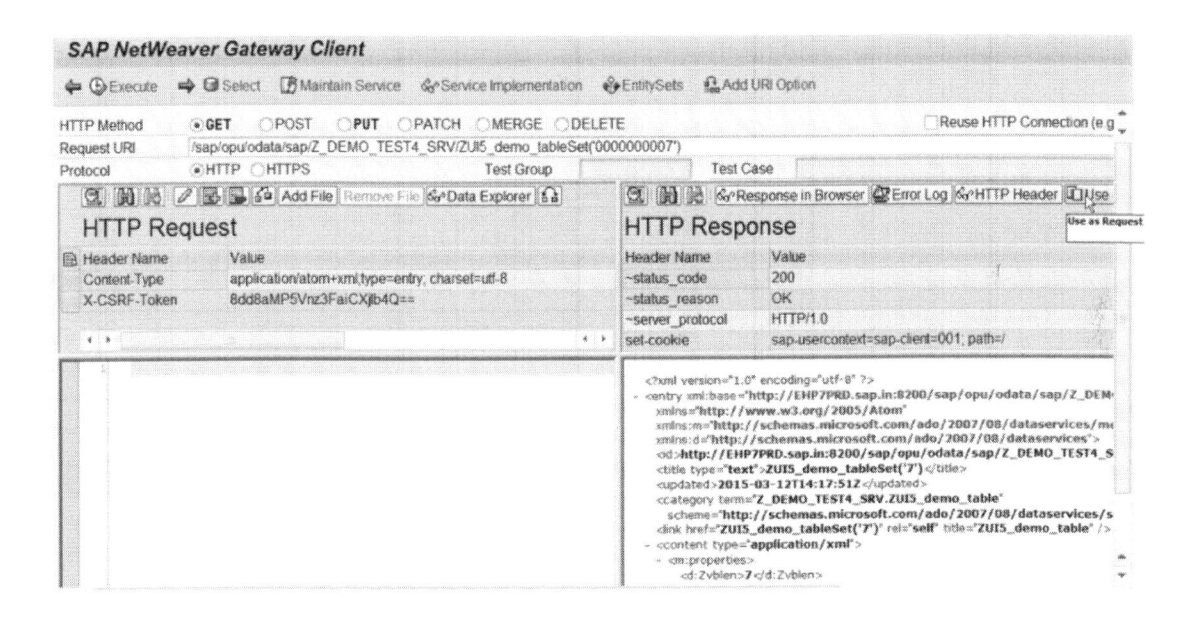

This is going to be our request which we will send to our server. We are going to update the name to "Jerry".

SAP® Netweaver Gateway

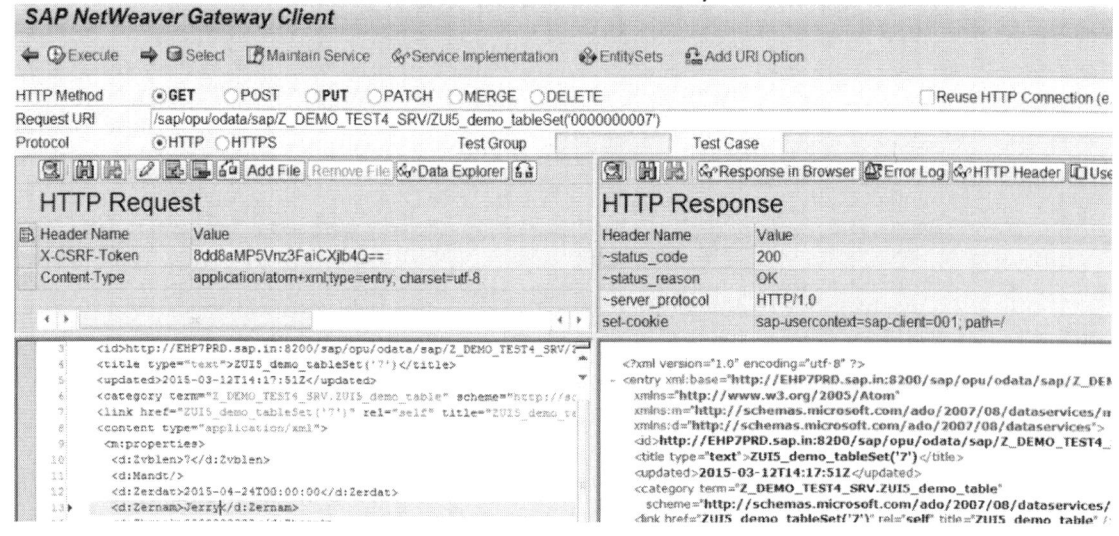

What my ABAP program tells now is that whatever data is passed in the body, read that table in ls_request_input_data and update that table accordingly where my ZVBLEN table field is equal to this data record.

So, based on the ZVBLEN field, we are going to update these table records with the new entries. This is a very simple ABAP program. You have to pass the key in URL from where the update should occur.

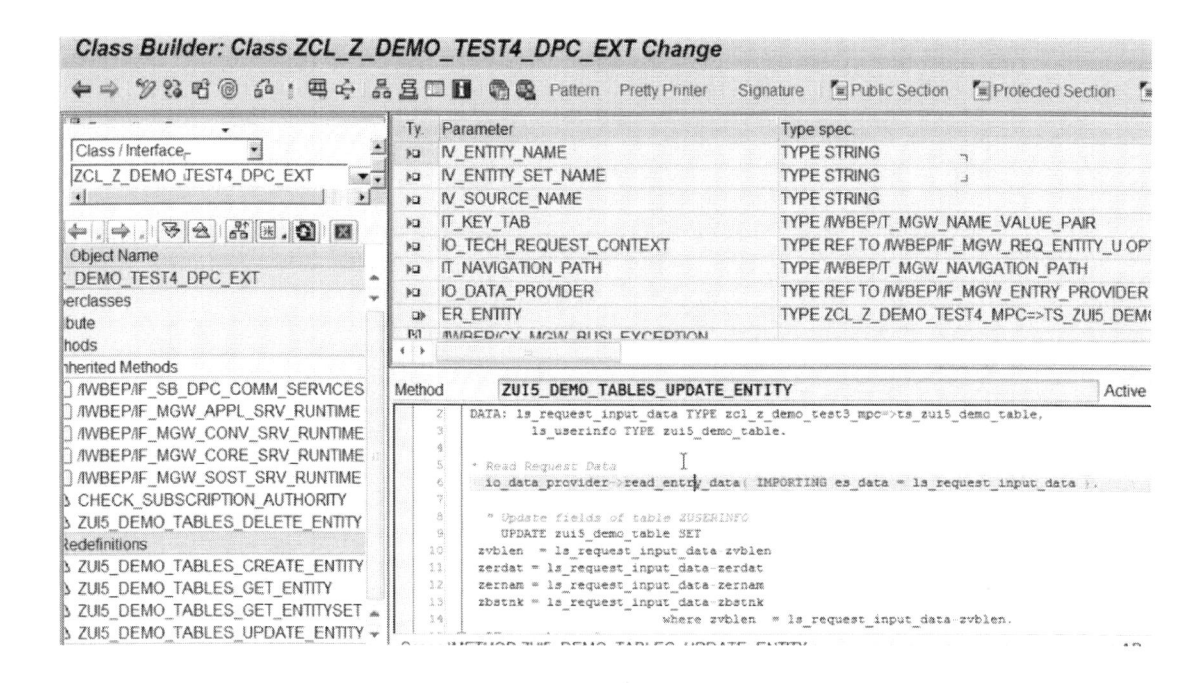

In this case, as we are using an Update, the HTTP method should be PUT.

Execute, and what we are expecting is that the name of the new record should be changed to "Jerry". We were successfully able to update the records. As we can see here, the response status is 204.

If we see our data browser to see the records, the name has changed to "Jerry". We have successfully implemented the Update operation.

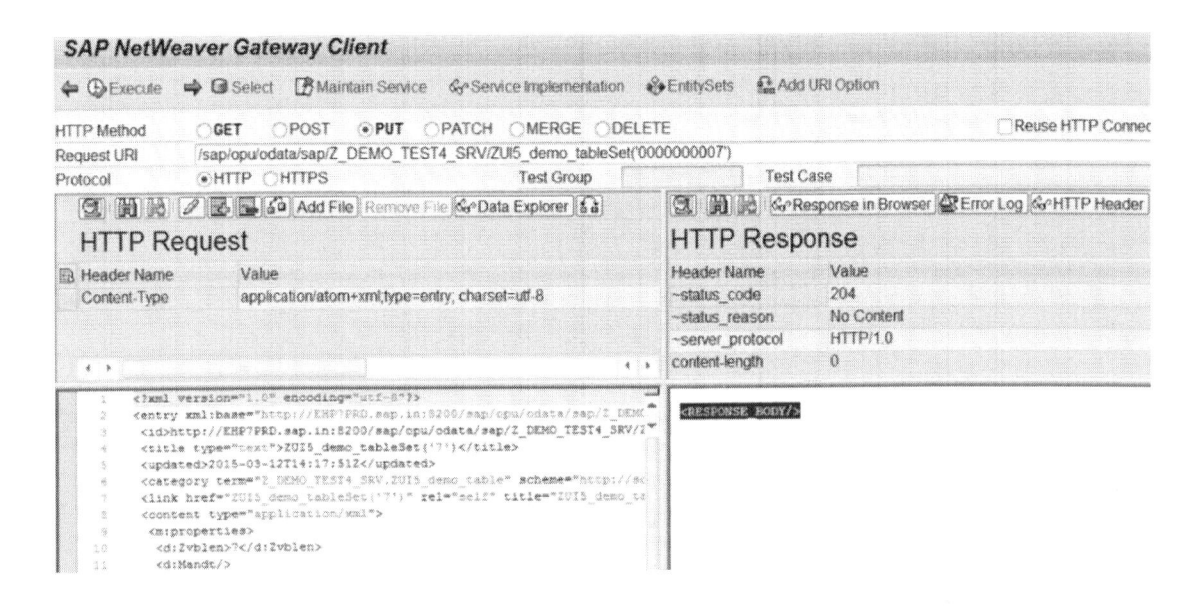

Let us put a debugging point here to show you what is happening inside.
Go to Gateway client and let's manually select a debugging point by writing /h, and Execute.

Now, we are able to go inside our debugging point which we set. We can see that this is the import parameter, and there is a method of this import parameter called read_entry_data.

You have to pass the structure ls_request_input_data to read this entry data, which is the same as when you created the service.

It will also depend on what response you sent to the service; that response body will be actually read here.

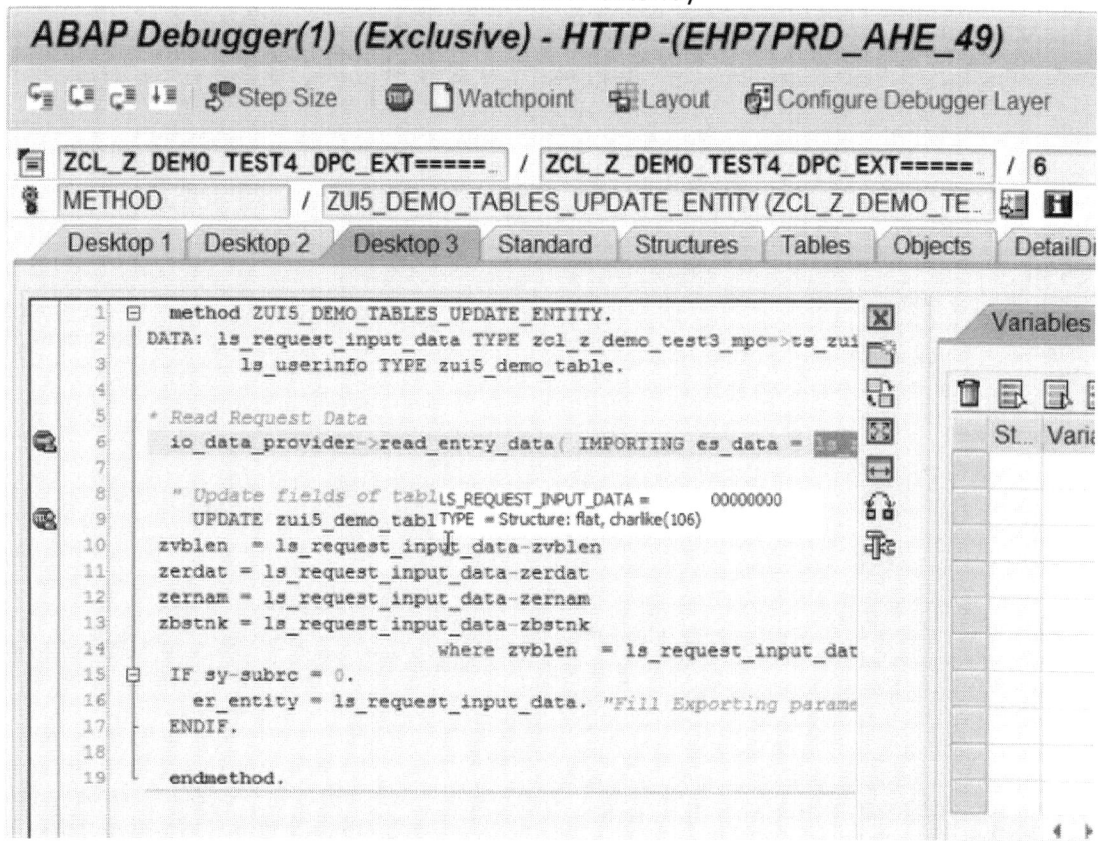

Switch to the next step and see what we got in the variable ls_request_input_data. You can see that our entire record will be there for "Jerry02".

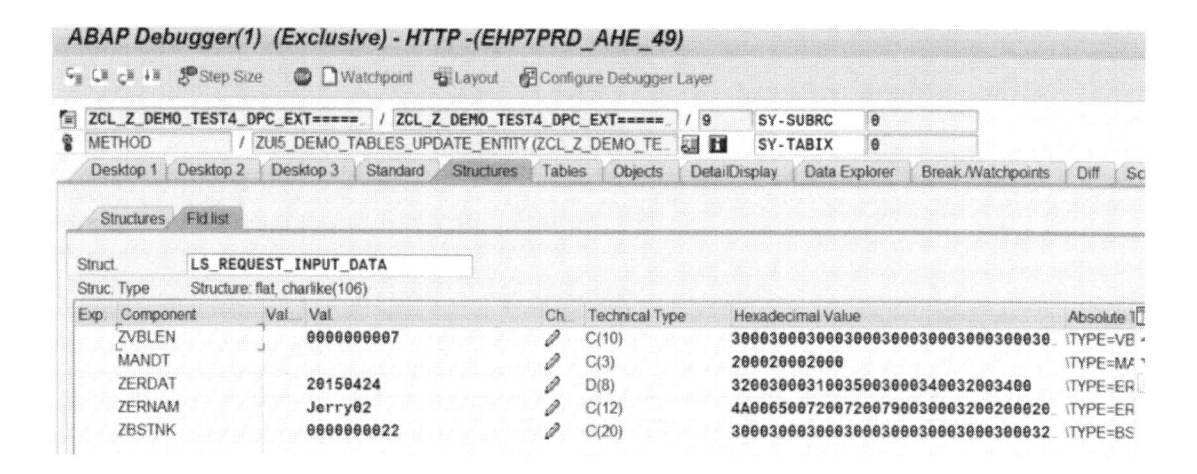

We are doing a simple Update query. We are updating zui5_demo_table, and setting all of the column values to the new record values which we got.

We are selecting a record from the ls_request_input_data, and zvblen is the key field which will tell which records to update.

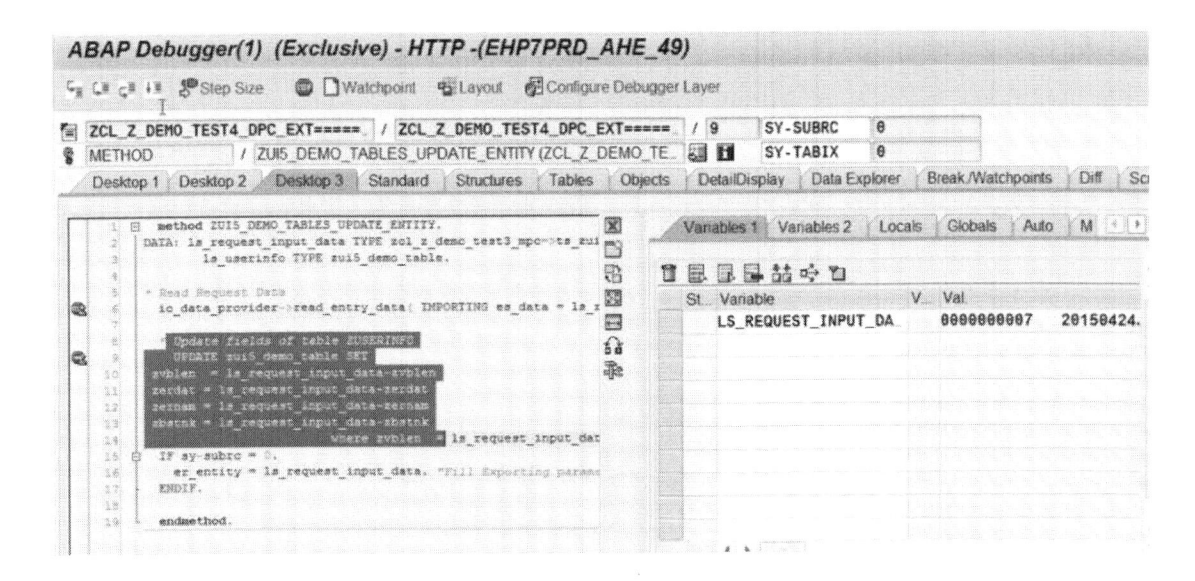

You can see that Update operation is working because when we try to finish this, we're getting a 204, the status code of success.

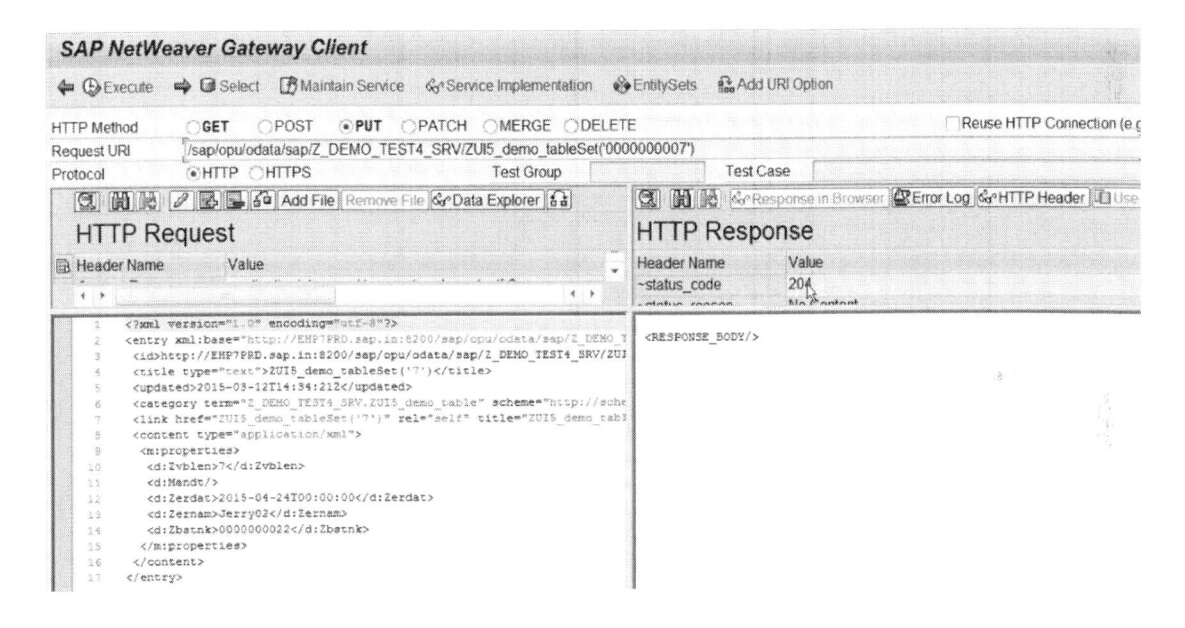

Let's go to se11, and see the records quickly. You can see that "Jerry02" is already updated.

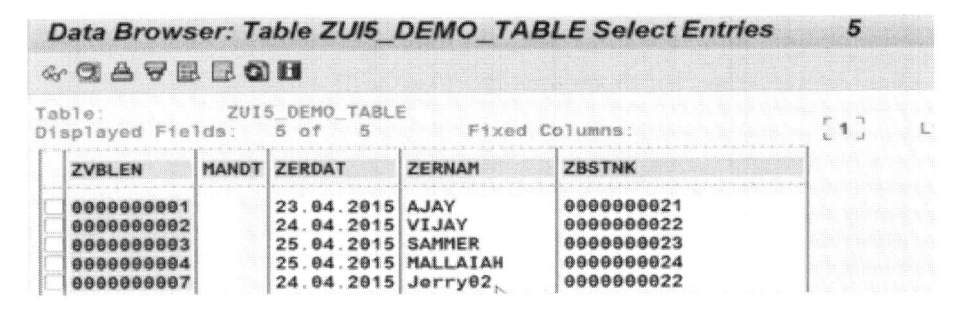

So this is how Update operation works.

2.6 Delete operation

C:Create   R:Read   U:Update   D:Delete   Q:Query

DELETE

Now the last one is the Delete operation, which is quite simple. We will be reading the same table in the same way we did for the Read operation. We will read the key, and we will delete the entry or the row where those keys exist.

These Delete, Update and Create operations should be ideally done by a function module if available. But for now, we will go to Class Builder, and Redefine the Delete method.

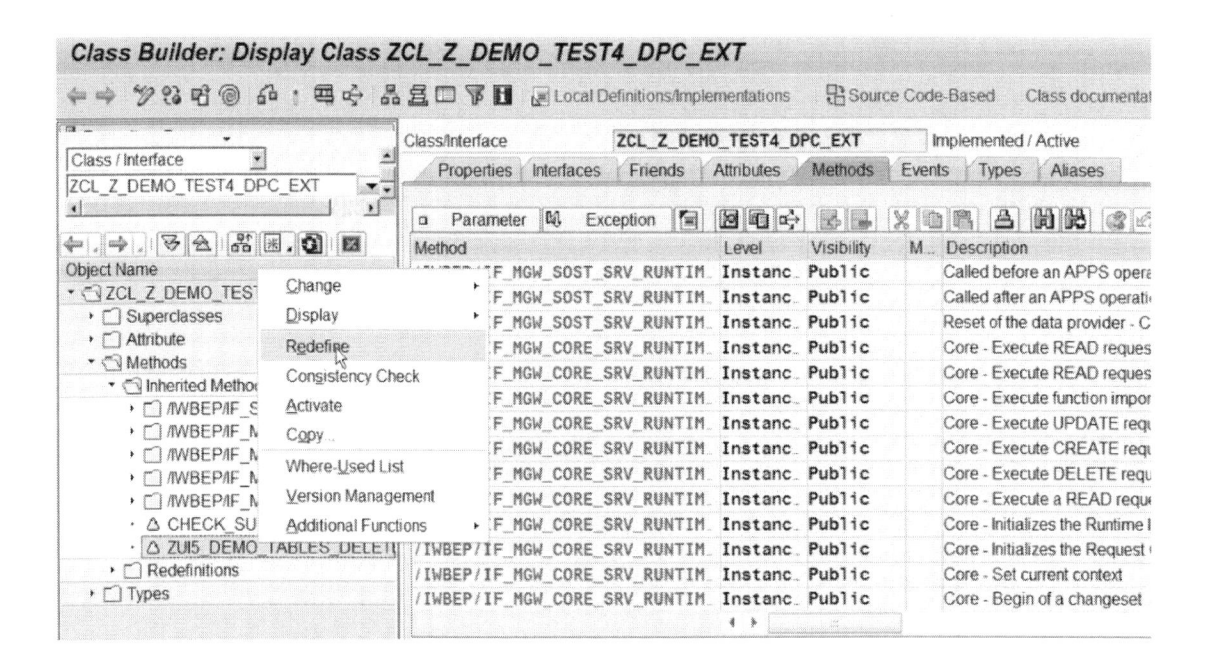

Let's copy our syntax here. Save and Activate it.

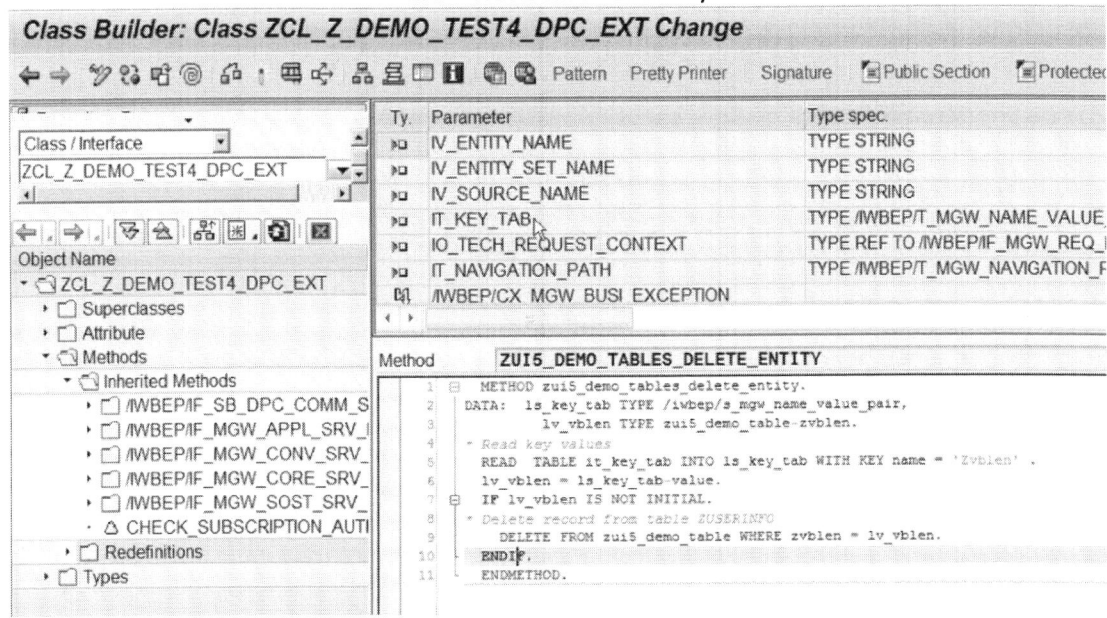

![Class Builder screenshot showing ZCL_Z_DEMO_TEST4_DPC_EXT class with method ZUI5_DEMO_TABLES_DELETE_ENTITY]

Zvblen is the key we read, and according to that key value, we will delete the record from the zui5_demo_table.

You can also have sy-subrc check. If it is not deleted, then there was some problem, and you can throw these exceptions.

For now, let us only Delete, and expect everything is going to be perfect. If not, then the internal exceptions will kick off and give us the error message. Let us Activate it.

```
DATA: ls_key_tab TYPE /iwbep/s_mgw_name_value_pair, lv_vblen TYPE
ZUI5_DEMO_TABLE-ZVBLEN.

* Read key values

 READ TABLE it_key_tab INTO ls_key_tab WITH KEY name = 'Zvblen' .

 lv_vblen = ls_key_tab-value.

 IF lv_vblen IS NOT INITIAL.

DELETE FROM ZUI5_DEMO_TABLE WHERE zvblen = lv_vblen.

ENDIF.
```

Let us go into the Gateway client. We are going to do the same thing. For example, if we do a GET, then we will get the record of the 7th number, which is the record of "Jerry02".

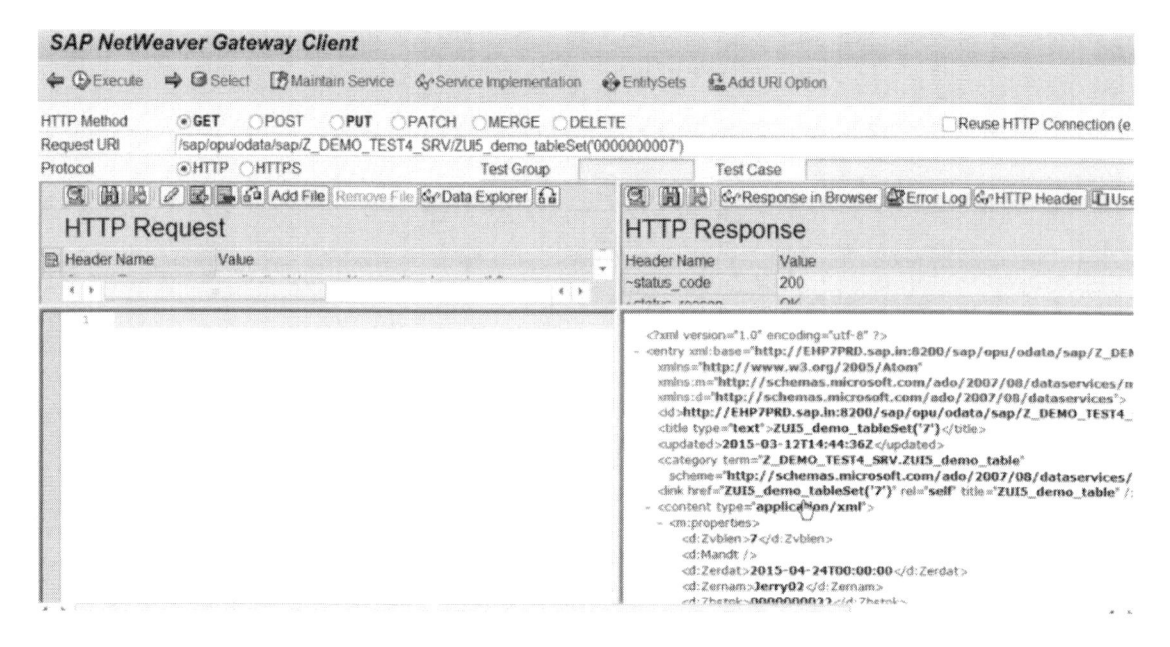

`/sap/opu/odata/sap/Z_DEMO_TEST4_SRV/ZUI5_demo_tableSet('0000000002')`

To delete this record, we just have to select the HTTP Method DELETE. Execute.

We can get a 204 success message, as the 200 series of response messages are of success series. That means my record would have been deleted.

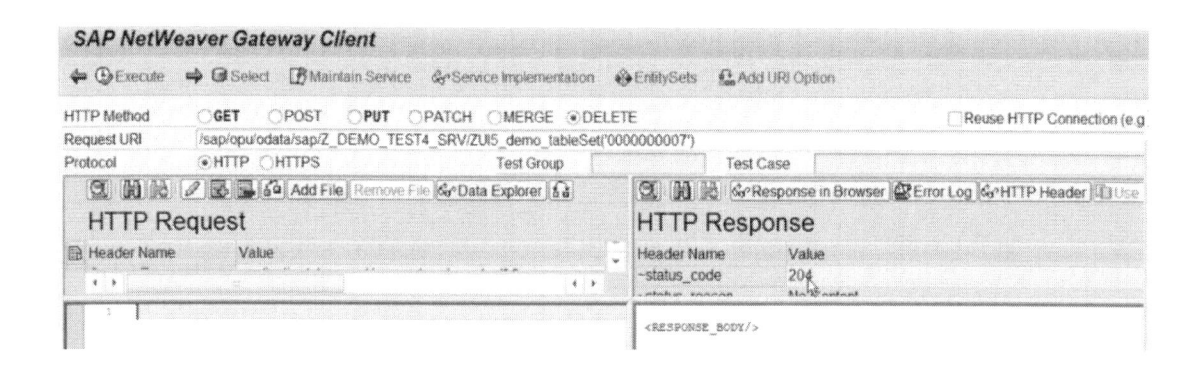

Let us check. Now, we can see in table that "Jerry02" is not there.

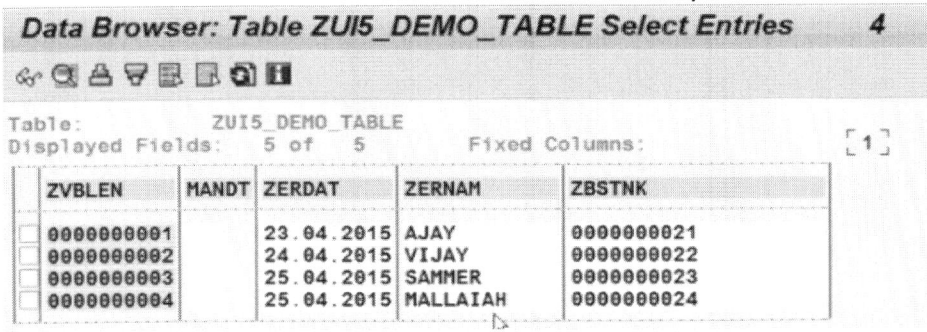

One way to check if your operation was done is by doing one more Read operation for that record. If you don't get any record anymore it will mean your Delete operation was successful.

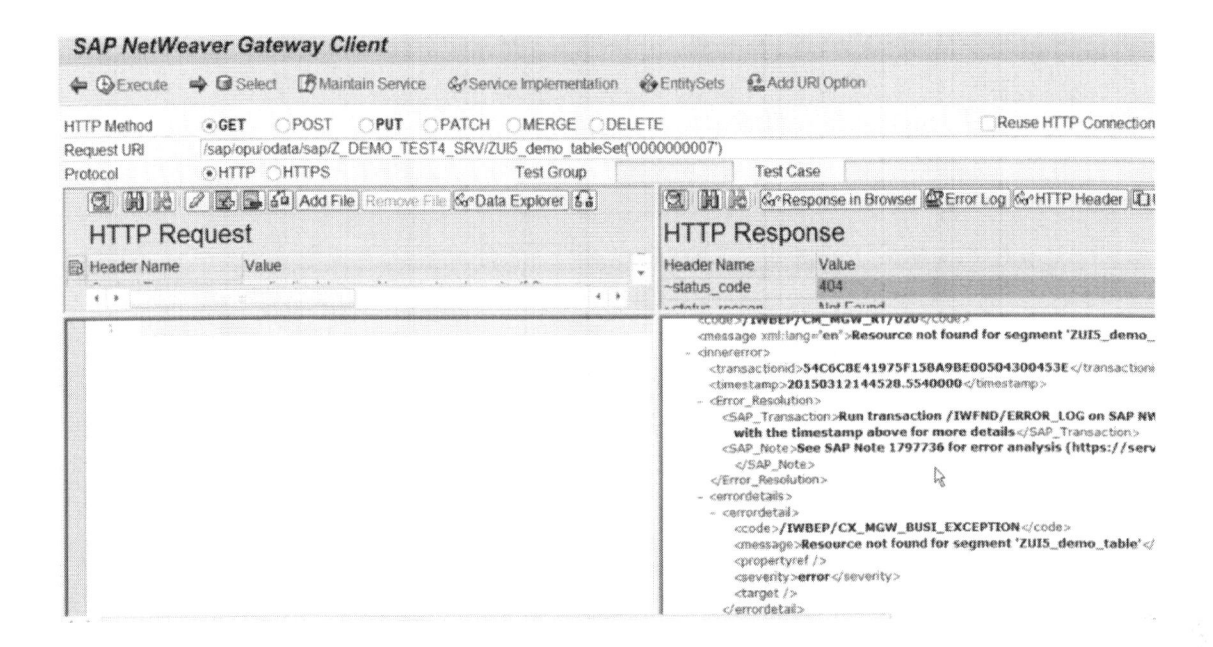

Now, we have successfully implemented the CRUDQ operations. Now only thing remaining is you have to expose those ABAP functionalities via NetWeaver Gateway to the outside world, in order to be used in SAPUI5 application.

Summary

In this section, we saw CRUDQ operation, where it stands for Create, Read, Update, Delete, and Query.
We implemented each one of them in SAP NetWeaver Gateway system step-by-step, and tested them in the gateway client and in web browser.

We also came to know the authentication mechanism for NetWeaver Gateway system while accessing the service from internet.

In the next section, we are going to see CRUDQ operation with SAP UI5 app. The procedure to access these services will be a bit different with UI5 app, so we will be going into details of how to use the services we have just created in the SAP UI5 app.

You can also, check our SAP NetWeaver Gateway course which demonstrates all the above CRUDQ operations steps in simple and easy to understand manner.
for the course coupon click here or use the QR code.

SAP Netweaver Gateway for SAPUI5, SAP Fiori and SAP HANA
UI5 Community Network , SAP Experts - SAP Services, SAP Consulting, SAP Education
20 € · ★★★★★ 4.2 (25 ratings) · 27 lectures, 3.5 hours video · All Levels

3. Integrating with SAP UI5 and deploying app

In this section, we are going to see how to implement our CRUD operation inside our SAP UI5 application.

3.1 Basic setup for SAPUI5 CRUD App

In the previous section, we saw how to create the CRUD operation, and we tested that in SAP NetWeaver Gateway Client. We also tested that in browser, but specifically, we didn't test the methods like Create, Update and Delete in the browser. This is because creating those scenarios using AJAX calls is a complicated task, as there are some security exceptions which you have to deal with when you do so.

There are some classes present inside the library which will make it a lot easier, and that would be the go-to method to use your Create, Update and Delete methods inside the SAP UI5 application.

Let's see the Gateway where we used to see the Update, Create and Delete processes, and where we actually copied the data.

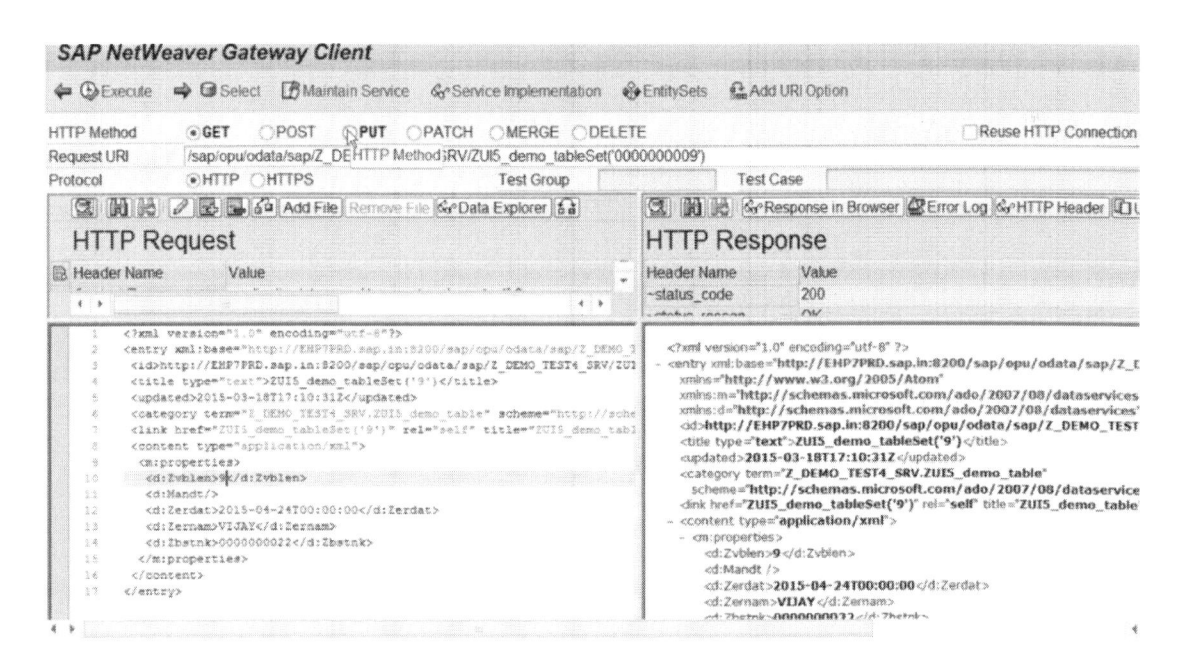

For example, if we GET the details, we can use this as request, we can change these values, and we can do a DELETE, or PUT operation. We have used PUT, POST, DELETE, and GET, where in the PUT was your Update, the POST was your

CREATE, the DELETE was your normal Delete, and the GET is used to Read the records.

Let us show the UI5 application which has already been built so we can test our scenarios.

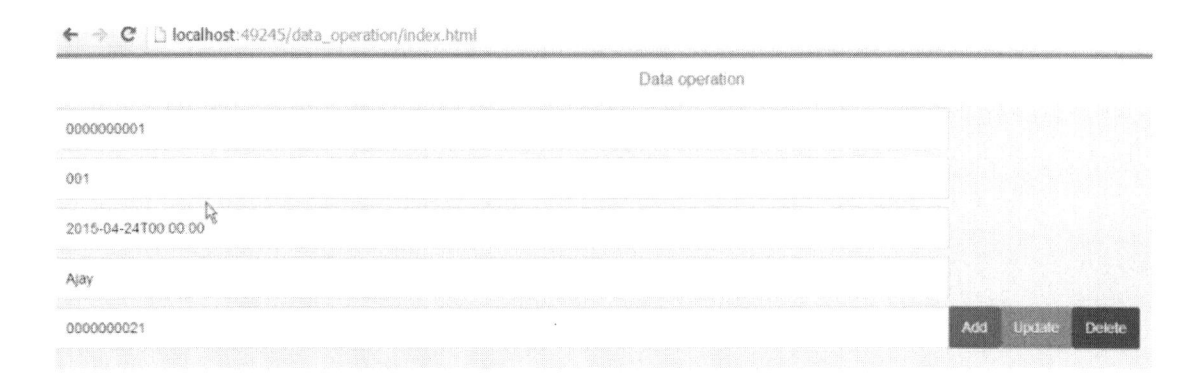

These are simple sap.m.Input boxes, and there are three sap.m.Buttons.

For example, let us create a new record, with the first entry as 0000000011. You can have labels before these input fields, but as we just wanted to show the CRUD operation, we didn't focus much on user experience.

Let us try to Add it, and see if we have a new entry with ZVBLEN as 0000000011, for the name "Ajay", and sales order number 0000000021, this time span and the client ID.

If we go to the table and refresh it, you will be able to see this newly created record.

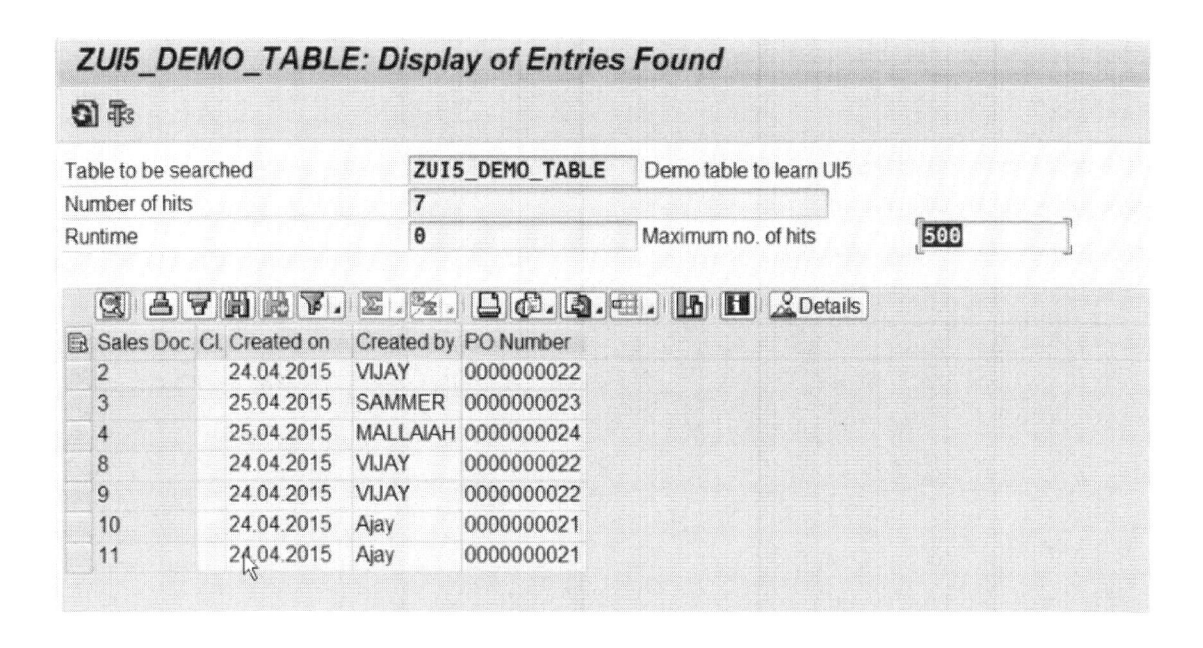

ZUI5_DEMO_TABLE: Display of Entries Found

Table to be searched	ZUI5_DEMO_TABLE	Demo table to learn UI5	
Number of hits	7		
Runtime	0	Maximum no. of hits	500

Sales Doc. Cl.	Created on	Created by	PO Number
2	24.04.2015	VIJAY	0000000022
3	25.04.2015	SAMMER	0000000023
4	25.04.2015	MALLAIAH	0000000024
8	24.04.2015	VIJAY	0000000022
9	24.04.2015	VIJAY	0000000022
10	24.04.2015	Ajay	0000000021
11	24.04.2015	Ajay	0000000021

Let us go back to the browser. If we want to change the name of the record to "Sammer", then we can do an Update here. If we go back and check the table we will find that it has been updated.

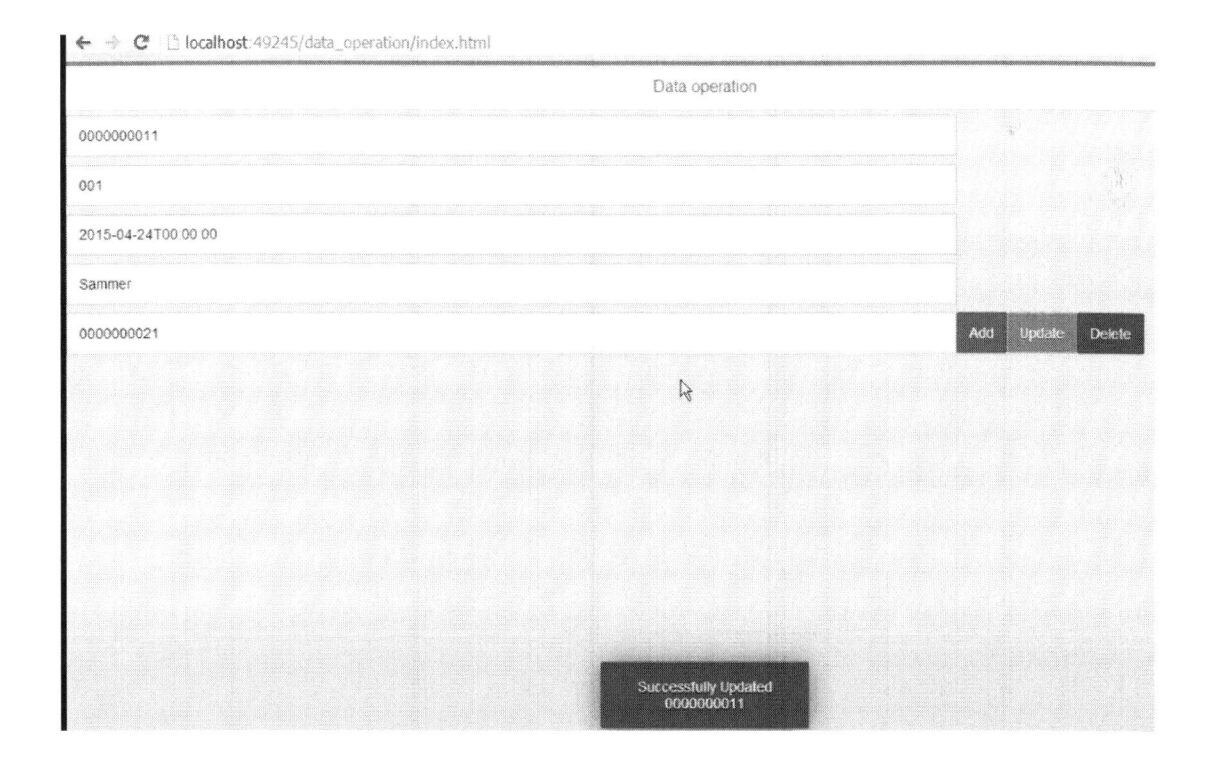

Data operation

0000000011

001

2015-04-24T00:00:00

Sammer

0000000021

[Add] [Update] [Delete]

Successfully Updated
0000000011

SAP® Netweaver Gateway
ZUI5_DEMO_TABLE: Display of Entries Found

Table to be searched	ZUI5_DEMO_TABLE	Demo table to learn UI5
Number of hits	7	
Runtime	0	Maximum no. of hits 500

Sales Doc. Cl	Created on	Created by	PO Number
2	24.04.2015	VIJAY	0000000022
3	25.04.2015	SAMMER	0000000023
4	25.04.2015	MALLAIAH	0000000024
8	24.04.2015	VIJAY	0000000022
9	24.04.2015	VIJAY	0000000022
10	24.04.2015	Ajay	0000000021
11	24.04.2015	Sammer	0000000021

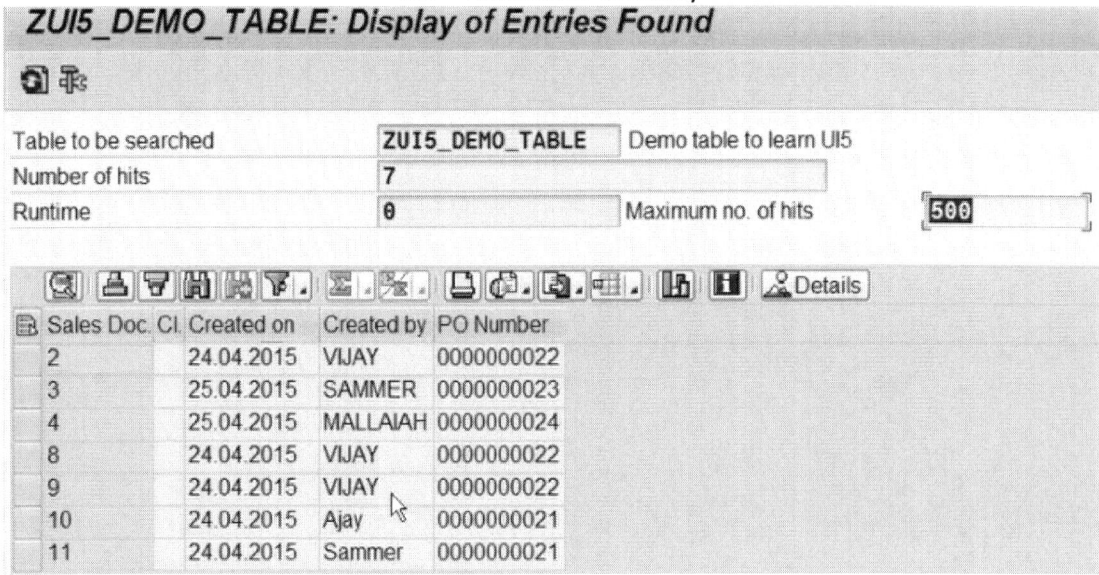

Now if we want to delete this record, we can just go ahead and Delete, and let's also verify that.

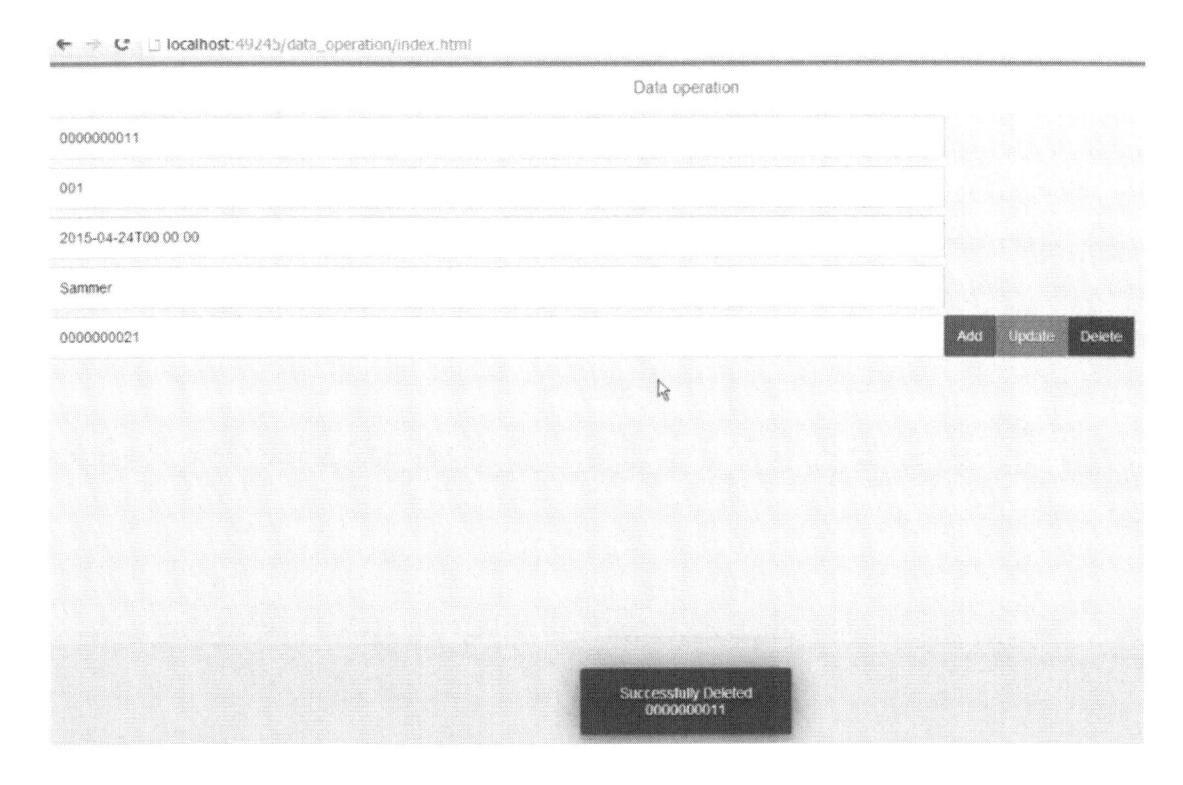

localhost:49245/data_operation/index.html

Data operation

0000000011

001

2015-04-24T00:00:00

Sammer

0000000021   Add   Update   Delete

Successfully Deleted
0000000011

If the record is not present, then it is because it has already been deleted. That is something that we need to do as a boundary test condition to see if those conditions or cases might arise in an application.

ZUI5_DEMO_TABLE: Display of Entries Found

Sales Doc. Cl.	Created on	Created by	PO Number
2	24.04.2015	VIJAY	0000000022
3	25.04.2015	SAMMER	0000000023
4	25.04.2015	MALLAIAH	0000000024
8	24.04.2015	VIJAY	0000000022
9	24.04.2015	VIJAY	0000000022
10	24.04.2015	Ajay	0000000021

Table to be searched: ZUI5_DEMO_TABLE — Demo table to learn UI5
Number of hits: 6
Runtime: 0
Maximum no. of hits: 500

We can go a lot fancier but for now let's stick to this simple usecase and see how these 3 features are implemented.

Let us go to Eclipse. Basically we are having SAP UI5 application. We have created an UI5 application with name data_operation. The index page is simple. We have one view page and one controller page, which are created by default.

index.html

```html
<!DOCTYPEHTML>
<html><head>
<metahttp-equiv="X-UA-Compatible"content="IE=edge">
<metahttp-equiv='Content-Type'content='text/html;charset=UTF-8'/>
<scriptsrc="resources/sap-ui-core.js"
                id="sap-ui-bootstrap"
                data-sap-ui-libs="sap.m"
                data-sap-ui-theme="sap_bluecrystal">
</script>
<script>
sap.ui.localResources("data_operation");
var app = new sap.m.App({initialPage:"iddemoCalls1"});
var page = sap.ui.view({id:"iddemoCalls1",
viewName:"data_operation.demoCalls",
type:sap.ui.core.mvc.ViewType.JS});
app.addPage(page);
app.placeAt("content");
</script>
    </head>
    <bodyclass="sapUiBody"role="application">
        <divid="content"></div>
    </body>
</html>
```

If you see the view page, there are 5 inputs and every one of them has an ID. These are the values which are displayed inside the input.

We have given the width, which is 70% of the webpage. There are only 3 buttons: Add, Update and Delete. This type is here to give the standard coloring of the buttons. After that, we have this press event so if the button is pressed, then it calls onSend from the controller, and it passes the Add parameter. This is the onSend function inside the controller page, and you can see that it has an sOperation.

demoCalls.view.js

```js
sap.ui.jsview("data_operation.demoCalls", {

    /**
     * Specifies the Controller belonging to this View. In the case that it is
     * not implemented, or that "null" is returned, this View does not have a
     * Controller.
     *
     * @memberOf data_operation.demoCalls
     */
    getControllerName : function() {
        return "data_operation.demoCalls";
    },

    /**
     * Is initially called once after the Controller has been instantiated. It
     * is the place where the UI is constructed. Since the Controller is given
     * to this method, its event handlers can be attached right away.
     *
     * @memberOf data_operation.demoCalls
     */
    createContent : function(oController) {
        return new sap.m.Page({
            title : "Data operation",
            content : [ new sap.m.Input("idZvblen", {
                    value : "0000000001",
                    width : "70%",
            }), new sap.m.Input("idMandat", {
                    value : "001",
                    width : "70%",
            }), new sap.m.Input("idZerdat", {
                    value : "2015-04-24T00:00:00",
                    width : "70%",

            }), new sap.m.Input("idZernam", {
                    value : "Ajay",
                    width : "70%",
            }), new sap.m.Input("idZbstnk", {
                    value : "0000000021",
                    width : "70%",
            }), new sap.m.Button({
                    text : "Add",
                    type : sap.m.ButtonType.Accept,
```

```
                    press : [ "Add", oController.onSend,
                                            oController ]
            }), new sap.m.Button({
                    text : "Update",
                    type : sap.m.ButtonType.Emphasized,
                    press : [ "Update", oController.onSend,
                                            oController ]
            }), new sap.m.Button({
                    text : "Delete",
                    type : sap.m.ButtonType.Reject,
                    press : [ "Delete", oController.onSend,
                                            oController ]
            }) ]
        });
    }

});
```

The "Add" value will be assigned to your sOperation and it will be passed while we are calling the onSend function.

demoCalls.controller.js

```
sap.ui.controller("data_operation.demoCalls",{

onInit :function() {

        $.ajax({
            type : "GET",
            url :
"http://<DNS/IP>:8200/sap/opu/odata/sap/Z_DEMO_TEST4_SRV/ZUI5_de
mo_tableSet/?$format=json",
            dataType : "json",
            headers : {
                "X-Requested-With" : "XMLHttpRequest",
                "Content-Type" : "application/atom+xml",
                "DataServiceVersion" : "2.0",
                "X-CSRF-Token" : "Fetch"
            },
            success : function(data, response, xhr) {

    sap.ui.getCore().setModel(xhr.getResponseHeader('x-csrf-
token'),
                                            "csrftoken");
            },
            error : function(error) {
                alert("Problem in connection");
                console.log(error);
            }
                });
    },
```

```javascript
onSend :function(evt, sOperation) {
        var oModel = new sap.ui.model.odata.ODataModel(
    "http://<DNS/IP>/sap/opu/odata/sap/Z_DEMO_TEST4_SRV/")
        var oData = {
            Zvblen : sap.ui.getCore().byId("idZvblen")
                    .getValue(),
            Zerdat : sap.ui.getCore().byId("idZerdat")
                    .getValue(),
            Zernam : sap.ui.getCore().byId("idZernam")
                    .getValue(),
            Zbstnk : sap.ui.getCore().byId("idZbstnk")
                    .getValue(),
        };

        if (sOperation === "Add") {
            oModel.create('ZUI5_demo_tableSet',
            oData,
            null,
            function() {
            sap.m.MessageToast
                    .show('Successfully added '
                    + oData.Zvblen);
            },
            function() {
            sap.m.MessageToast
                    .show('Error in Adding new record');
            });

        } elseif (sOperation === "Update") {
oModel.update('ZUI5_demo_tableSet(\''+ oData.Zvblen + '\')',
            oData,
            null,
            function() {
            sap.m.MessageToast
                .show('Successfully Updated '
                            +    oData.Zvblen);
                },
                function() {
                    sap.m.MessageToast
                    .show('Error in Updating record');
                });
        } elseif (sOperation === "Delete") {
        oModel.remove('ZUI5_demo_tableSet(\''
                + oData.Zvblen + '\')', null, function() {
            sap.m.MessageToast.show('Successfully Deleted '
                    + oData.Zvblen);
        }, function() {
            sap.m.MessageToast
                    .show('Error in Updating record');
        });
        } else {
        }
    }
});
```

You can see here in controller that we are having an AJAX in onInit method whenever the application initializes. This will be loaded at the beginning when you start the application.

This is because whenever we are doing an AJAX call, which is in GET in this case, to some service to read some records, it will ask us for username and password.

We will get a standard pop-up message. Once you give your username and password there, all the other calls will not require any more accesses as they will be using the same credentials. In the same application, if there are more calls, they will all be using the same authentication.

You can see that we are actually setting the model. We are having a CSRF token here. We are actually passing the headers X-CSRF-Token fetch. We have to store your CSRF token in your model or as a variable.

We won't see how to implement this operation using normal AJAX call because that is very complicated, and is also not advisable in your UI5 application to have normal AJAX calls for your Update, Create, and Delete operations. You will see the normal way that will be used in your application. In a nutshell, these AJAX calls are only used to get you authorized.

After that, in the onSend function, according to your parameter it can either be add, update or delete, to do this specific operation.

We store all the data values inside a JSON object called oData. We have keys called ZVBLEN, ZERDAT, ZERNAM, and ZBSTK.

To get these, go to the NetWeaver Gateway Client, and you filter it with $format=json. Execute this, and copy.

These are all the key fields, and you can copy the exact character types here, as the capital and small letters should be taken care of, and should be mentioned as it is.

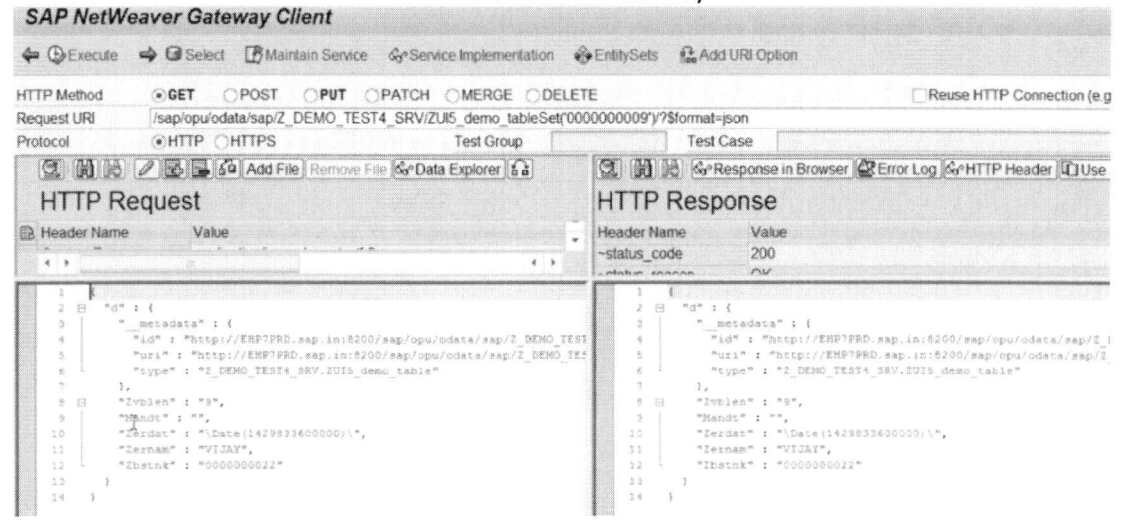

The "0000000009" here is only "9", but you have to pass the leading zeros as well because this is VBLEN field type. That is something which is mandatory for that particular data element to be updated or created.

In the beginning, we are having an oModel. This is the standard class which you will be using to get an access to an object which has all capabilities to create, update and remove.

If you go to browser, and open this documentation of SAP UI5, you can see that the class sap.ui.model.odata.ODAtaModel has many functions like remove, refresh, and create. We will be using this class and the functions present inside this class. This is advisable when you are doing a UI5 application for those

> **Note: Service Prefix**
>
> http://<DNS/IP>:<port>/sap/opu/odata/sap/ is the prefix which we have to add before the service name. Here DNS/IP is the DNS address or IP address of you SAP ERP system and port is integer number in which the services are running. This prefix can change depending upon system

operations like Create, Update, & Delete.

Once we get this object, we have to pass this service URL:

```
http://<DNS/IP>:<port>/sap/opu/odata/sap/Z_DEMO_TEST4_SRV/
```

After that, the service name is Z_DEMO_TEST4_SRV. This is the URL which will be put in this ODataModel, and get access to all operations like create, update, and remove or delete.
Inside the controller, you see that it has a sOperation. Once we pass this sOperation, you just call these URLs that we saw in the Gateway.

Let us go back to the Gateway client. After this service URL, we are passing this particular string. If you see the previous sections, this part was different. This will be the first parameter for your oModel.

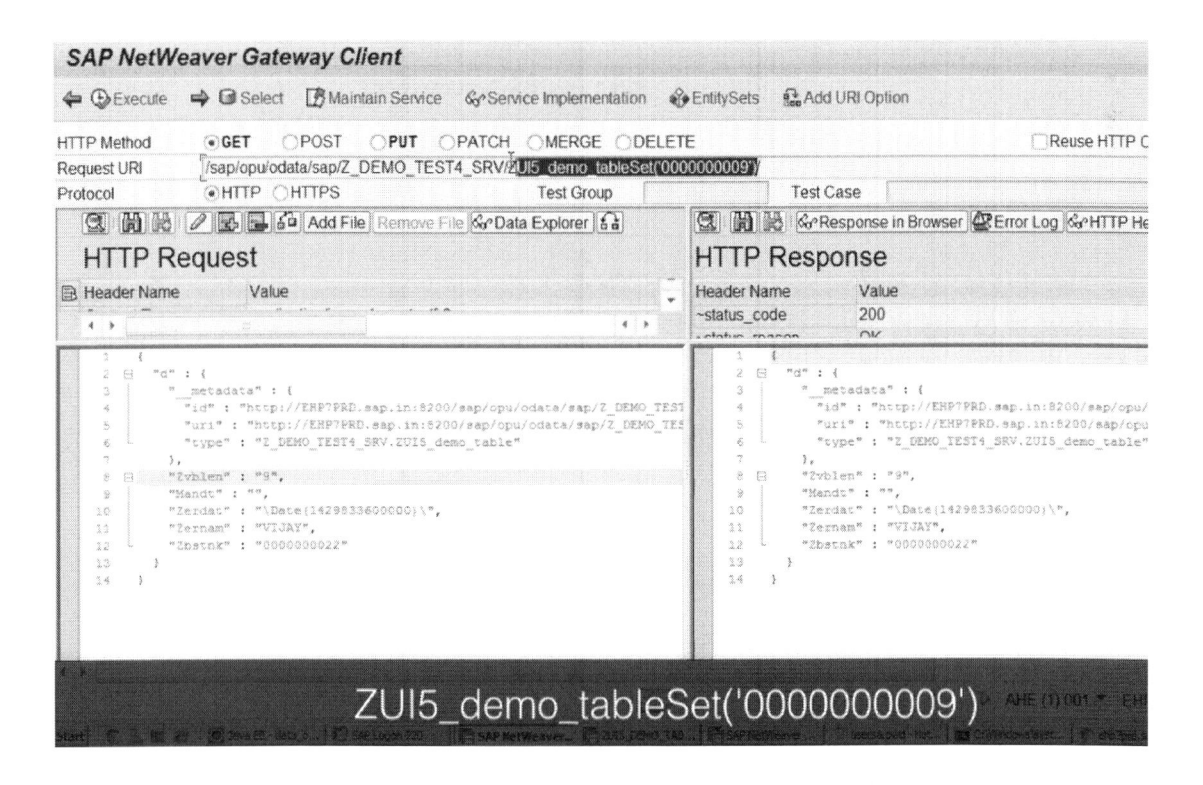

When we create, we only pass Set. When we update, we pass Set and the particular value that should be updated. When we delete, we also pass the Set with the key parameter that should be removed.

The next parameter will be the data, which is required in the create and update processes. In the delete or remove process, we don't require data because it will just delete according to the key you have provided.

After that is a null parameter, followed by two functions: if you have functionSuccess, then the first function is executed; and, if it is functionFailure, then the second function will be executed. This is the same throughout the create, update and remove processes.

We are using an sap.m. MessageToast, which is a small popup that appears for about 3 seconds, and says the record is successfully created, updated or deleted.

This is something which we will be seeing again while in our browser. This is how UI5 application or implementation is being made. It just takes the filled values and, according to which button we press, it executes the specific function of our model.

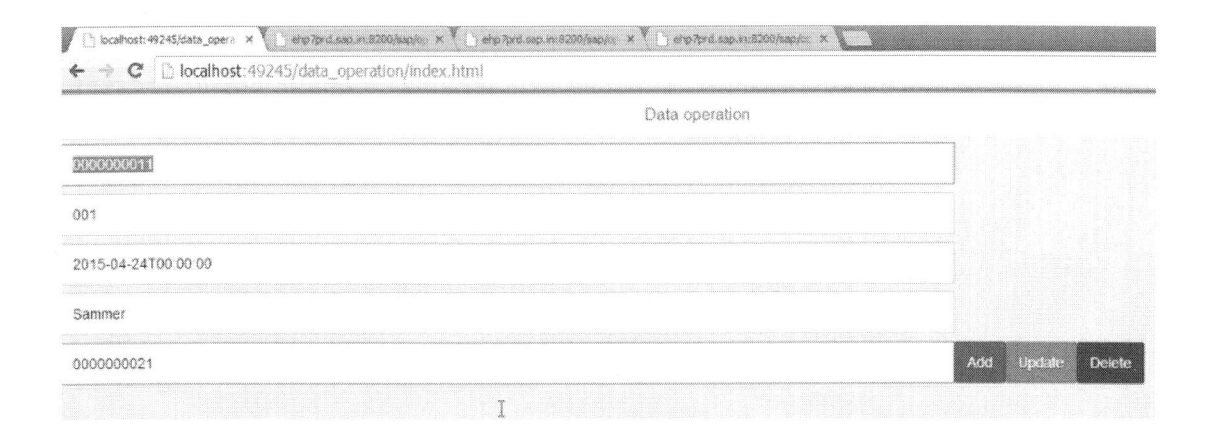

There are few things to remember here. The first is that you should not start your Chrome browser directly from the Desktop, because you are doing a local development. If you want to do an AJAX operation to a server from your local host, then it will not be allowed in the Chrome.

You have to open Chrome in a security-disabled mode. To do that, right-click on the Chrome icon, and select Properties. Copy the location of your Chrome application, and change your directory to that particular location on cmd.exe. Write this special command:

```
chrome.exe –disable-web-security
```

Sometimes, this creates a lot of confusion. Your AJAX calls are not working because your browser will not allow your server calls from your local host, so you have to disable your web security.

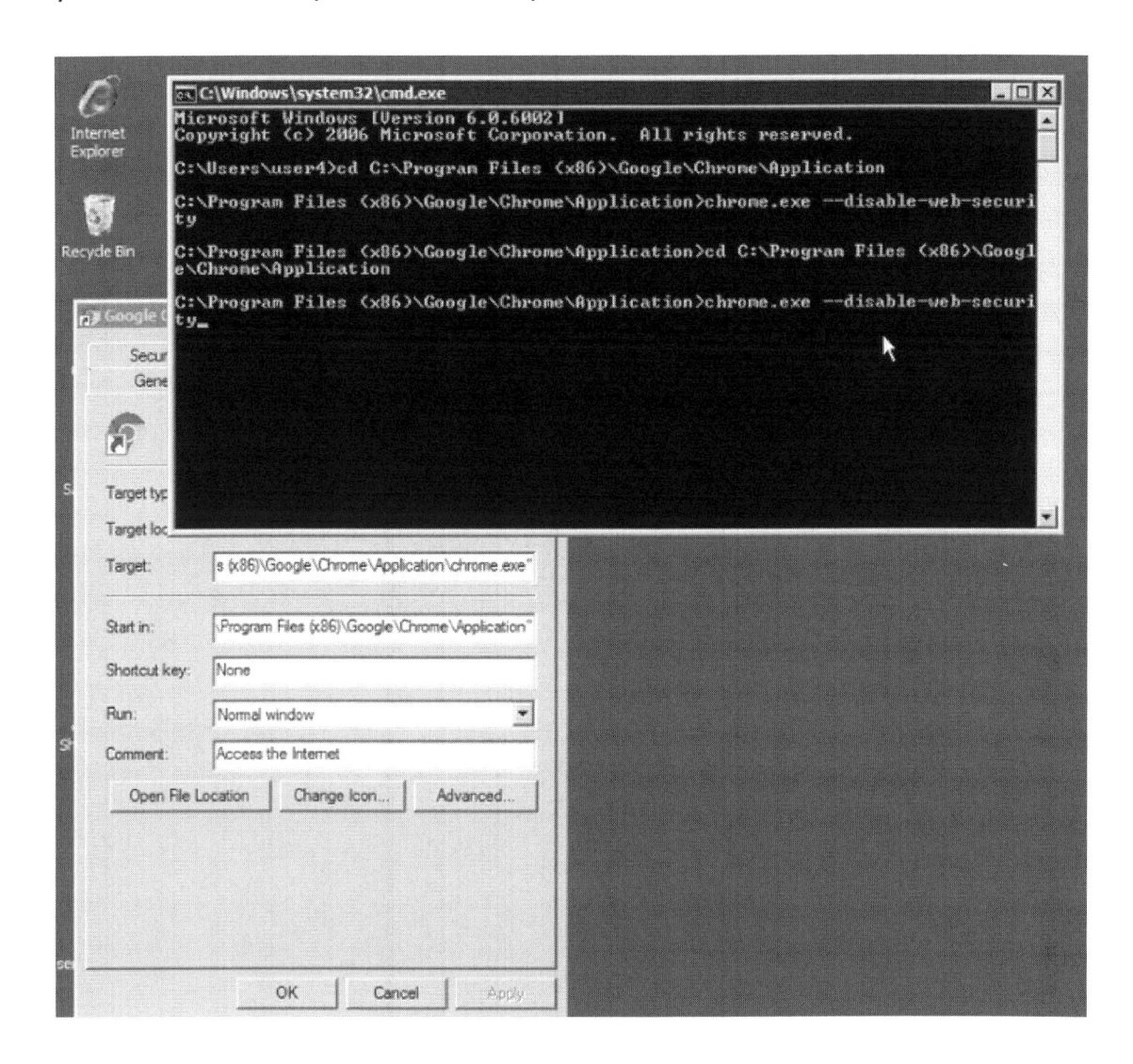

This is something you have to do in Chrome. Firefox will work fine without disabling the web security.

Let us open the Eclipse, and copy the URL of the application which we are seeing in the browser.

This is the challenge method because we wrote one GET function call in the init() method. This will allow us to get authorized from SAP. This is the standard SAP login, and we have to give the username and password.

SAP® Netweaver Gateway

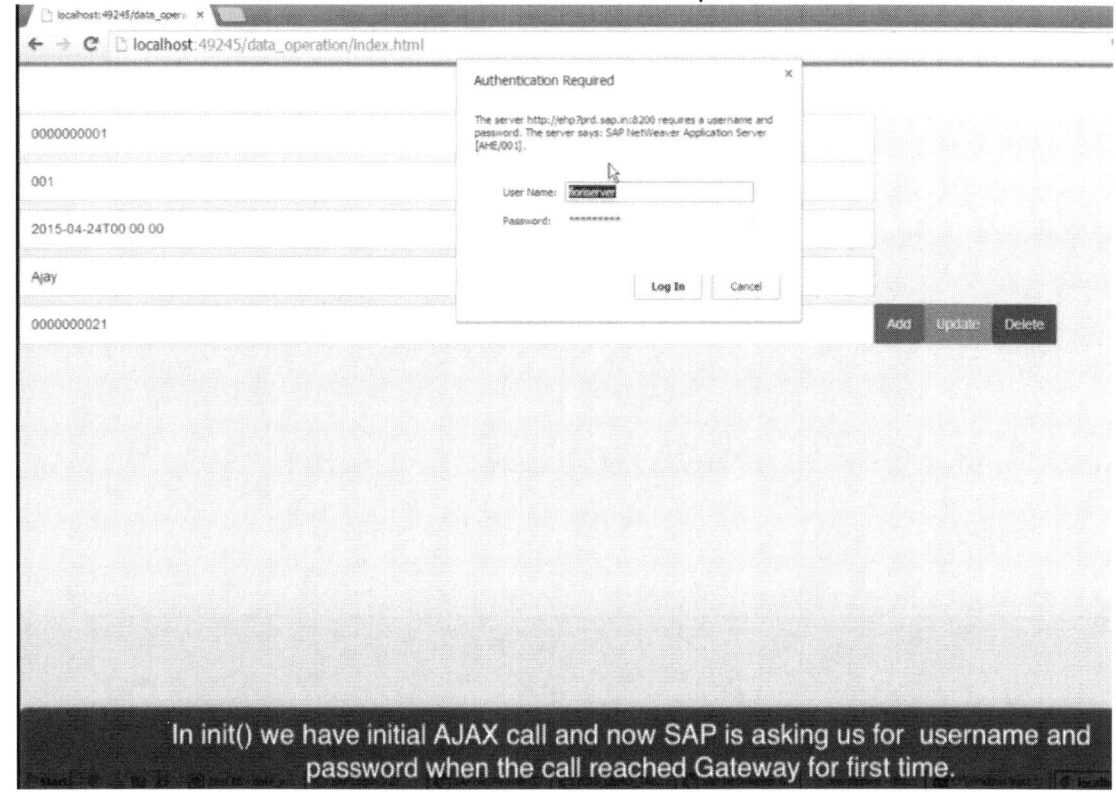

In init() we have initial AJAX call and now SAP is asking us for username and password when the call reached Gateway for first time.

To put it in a simple way, this call which we do in the init() is there to get authorized initially. Once you are authorized by your backend, then you will be able to do all other operations like create, update, and delete. You need to get authorized once.

We can get authorized even by calling the URL in a new browser, like the incognito mode, for example.

Now that we are authorized, our files have the information of authentication, so that the next time we do a call, it will not ask for any more username and password for this particular session.

The same thing happens for the first time opening the application. You will be challenged and your credentials will be taken, and all operations are performed with that authentication. To do this operation, we are using this type of oModel: sap.ui.model.odata.ODataModel.

There will be issues when you are dealing with these services. If you get errors, the best way is to look at the Gateway and go to the transaction

/IWFND/ERROR_LOG to see all errors which have occurred. Click on the time stamp, and you can get all the details below Error Context.

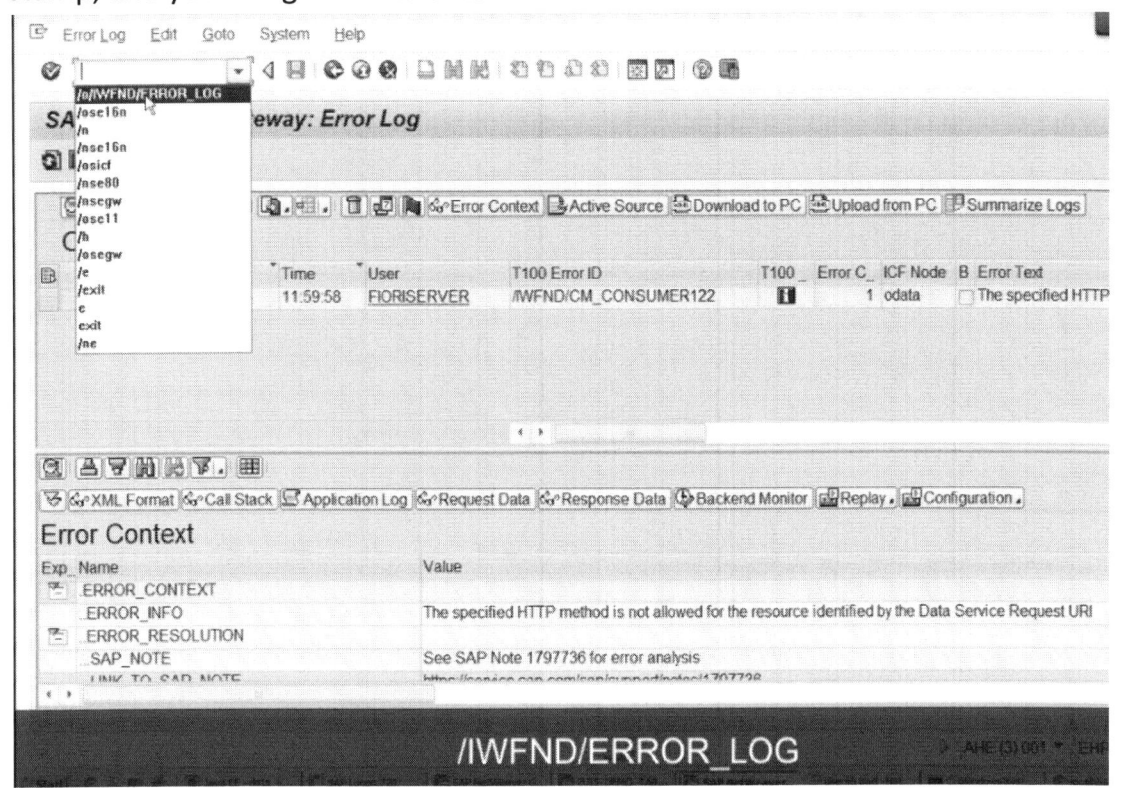

The key of the table is Zvblen. You can see here that we are putting a \'. This is because when we want a new URL, we cannot write " because it stands for end of the string in the javascript. Therefore, use \' which is called an escape sequence. To make ' appear in the string, we have to use an escape sequence in the beginning and in the end of the key parameter.

In the Chrome browser, if you go to Inspect Element and to the Network tab, and try to do an update, you will see that your URL looks like this:

```
http://<DNS/IP>:<port>/sap/opu/odata/sap/Z_DEMO_TEST4_SRV/ZUI5_demo_ta
bleSet('0000000014')
```

SAP® Netweaver Gateway

When you are doing this kind of development, you will be going into Console many times, to test some snippets and try a lot of things.

Now, if we try to delete this record, the same thing will happen – you will be passing the oModel for deleting this key, and it will be deleting the record. Once you have entire app set up, you can also push this code to SAP.

3.2 Sharing SAPUI5 Project into SAP

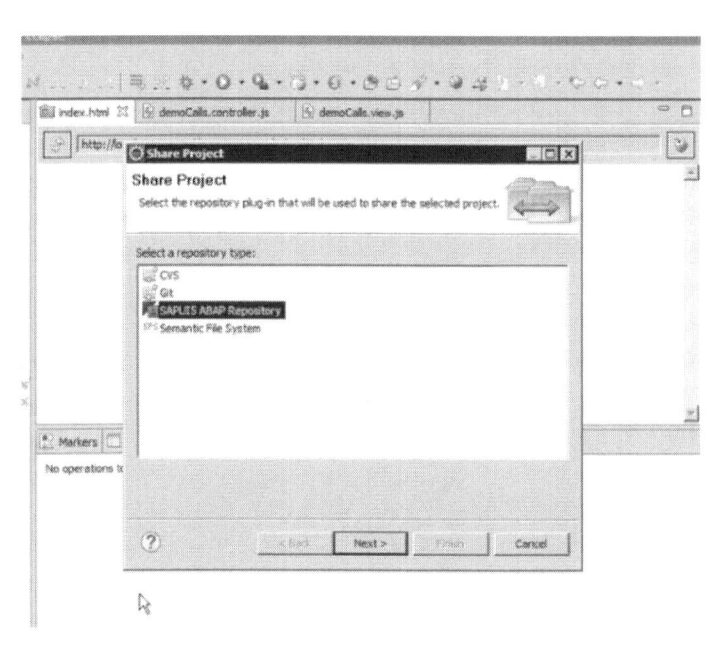

In eclipse, right-click on data_operation, go to Team and select Share Project. Select which SAP system where we want to push the UI5 code.

SAP® Netweaver Gateway

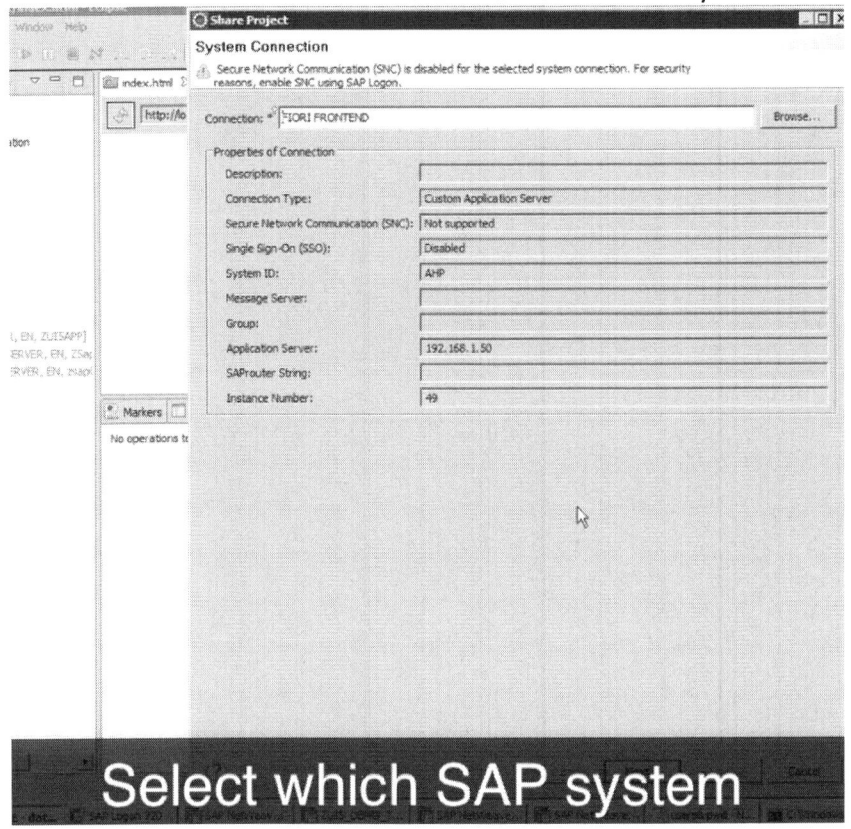

Select which SAP system

It will ask for the client, username and password for the SAP logon.

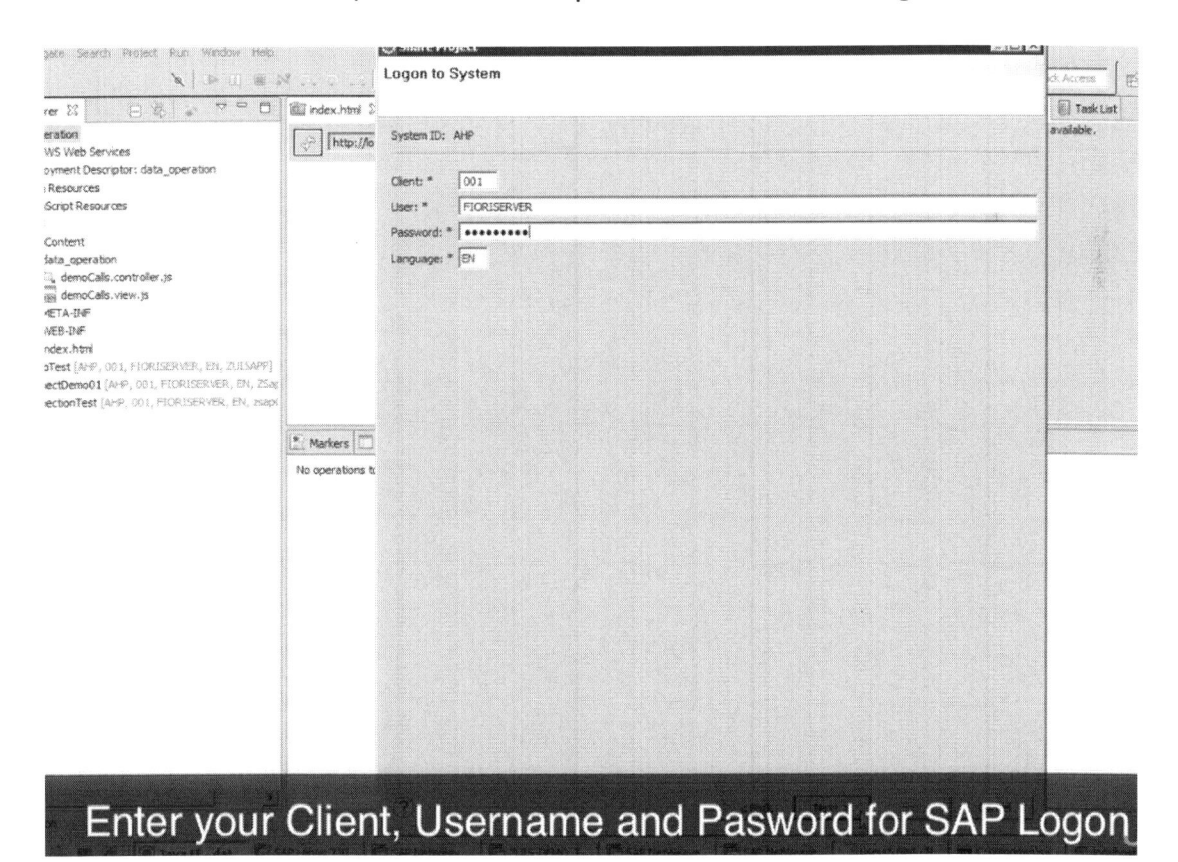

Enter your Client, Username and Pasword for SAP Logon

After that, we will be selecting the BSP application. If you have any BSP application, then you can filter it from here, or you can create a new BSP application.

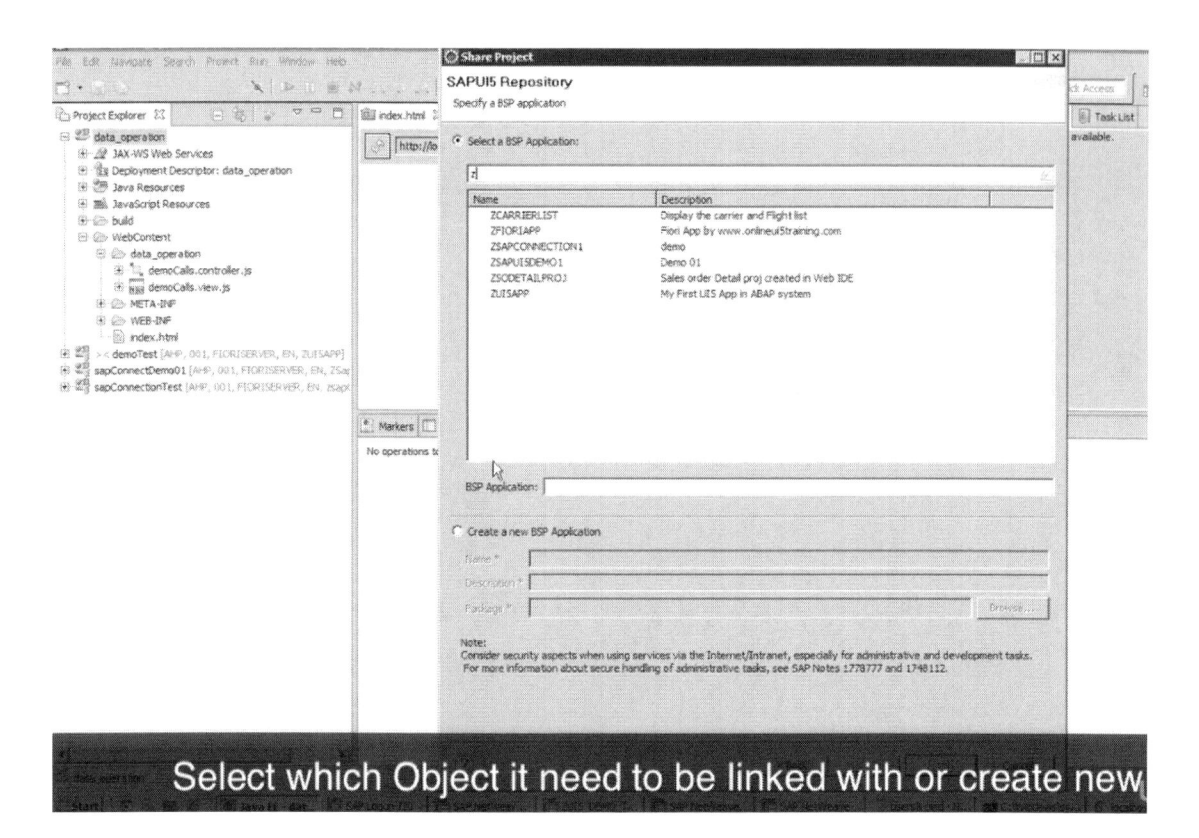

Select which Object it need to be linked with or create new

We will create a new BSP application for this demonstration. Let us give the name, description and the package. If you have any existing package, you can manually type it in, or you can filter as well. Let us use $TMP to make it a local object. After that click Finish.

> **Note: Local Object**
>
> Local objects (Dev class $TMP) areindependent of correction and transport system.So we use $TMP very frequently for objects which are created for testing purpose in development systems.

$TMP will make the object a local object

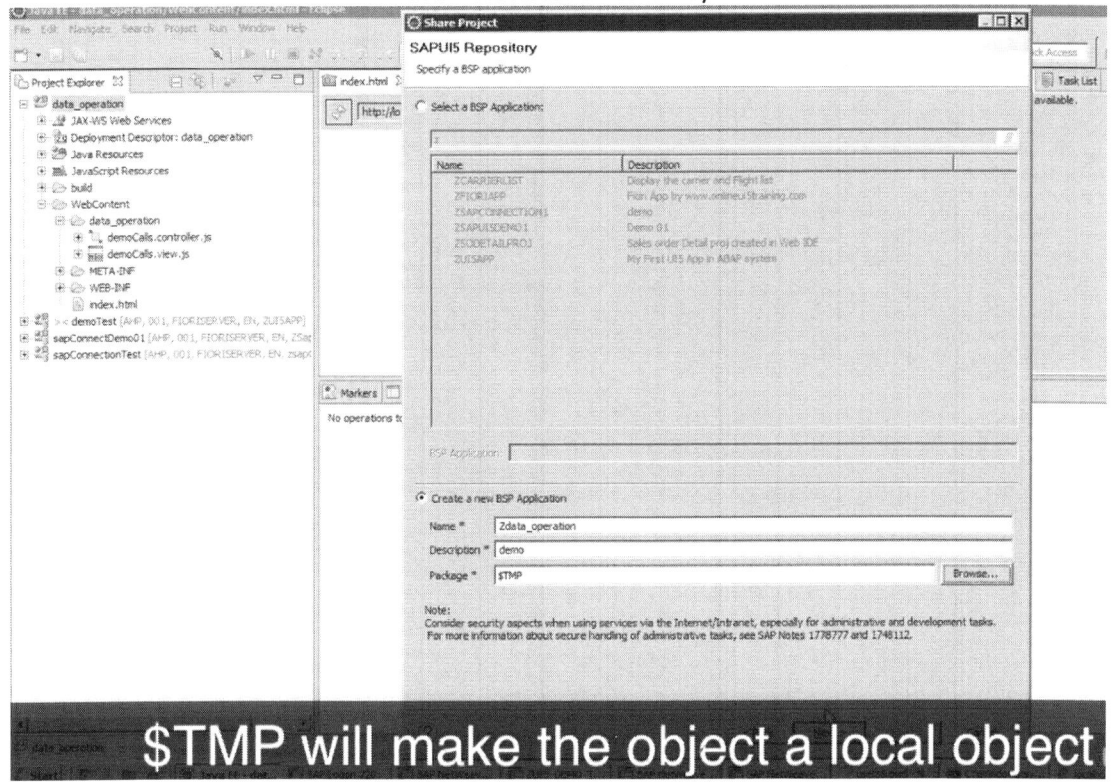

Now, we have successfully created this project inside our SAP.

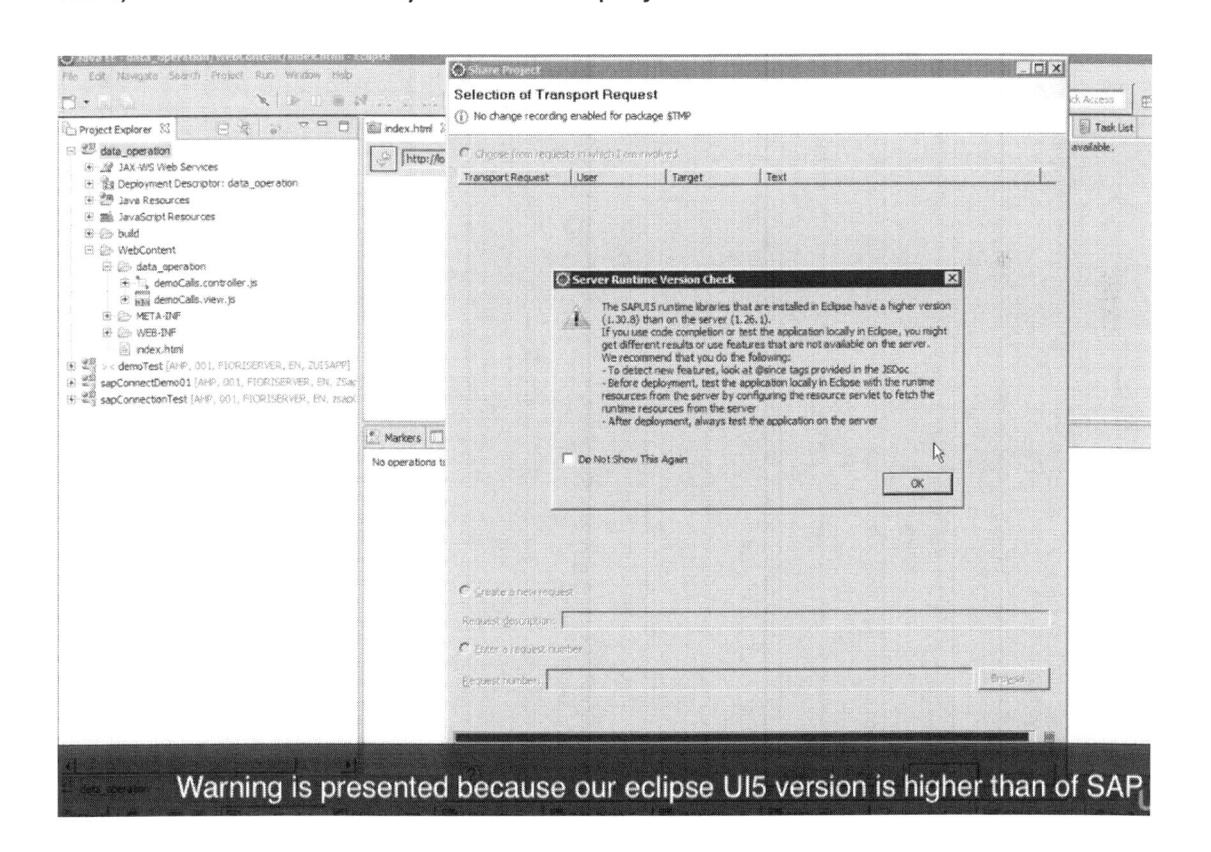

Warning is presented because our eclipse UI5 version is higher than of SAP

We will push our shared project. Right-click on data_operation, go to Team and select Submit. Select all the files which will be shared to SAP, then click Finish.

85

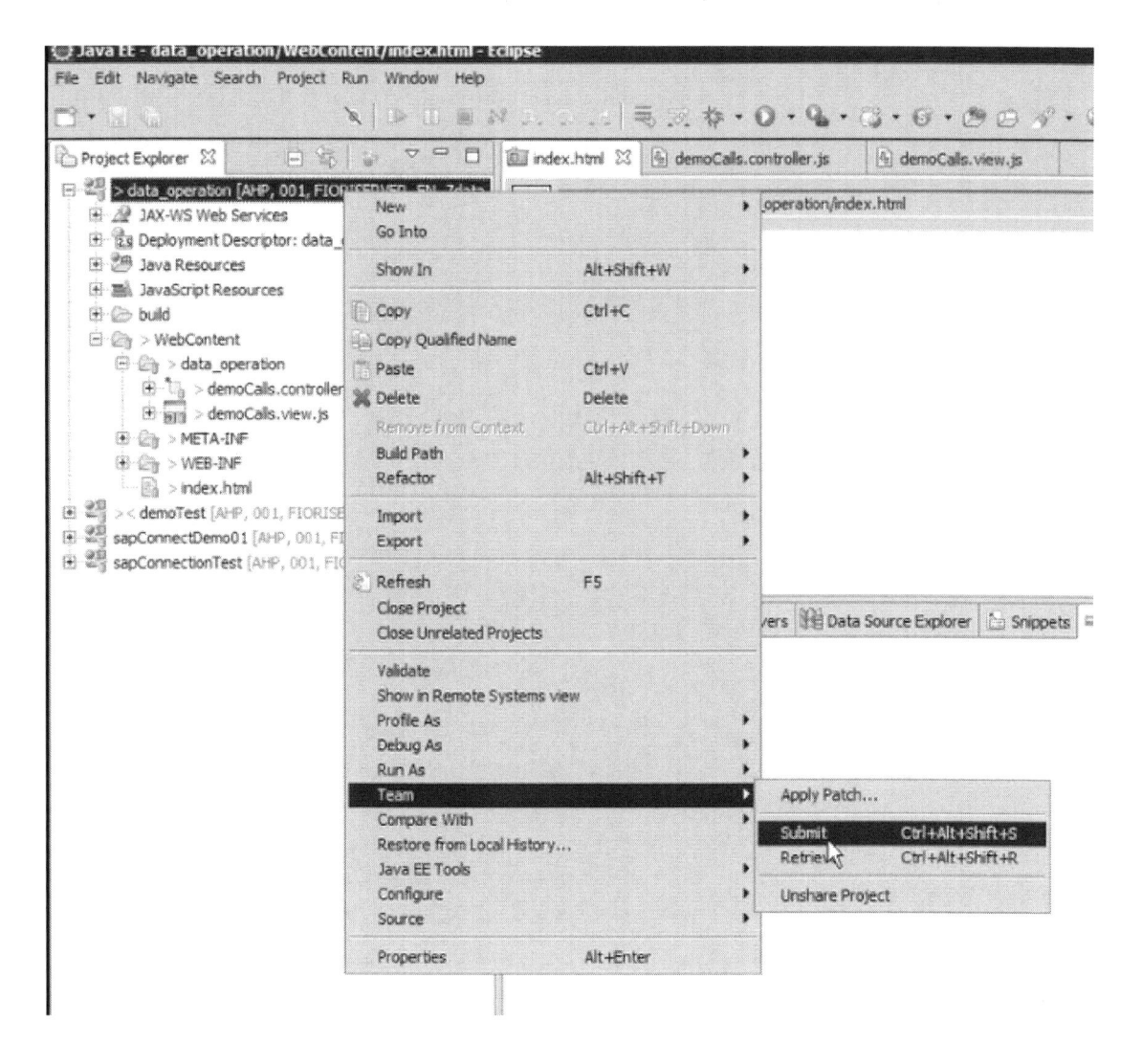

Go to the SE80 transaction, and go inside the BSP application. Select the object name which we just pushed (ZDATA_OPERATION).

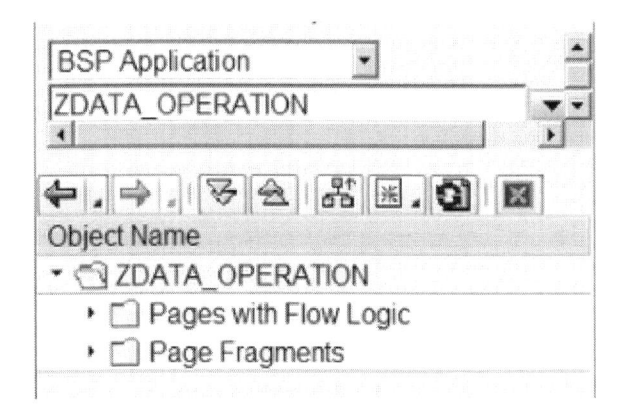

Let's try to run our application. Navigate to the index page and test it.

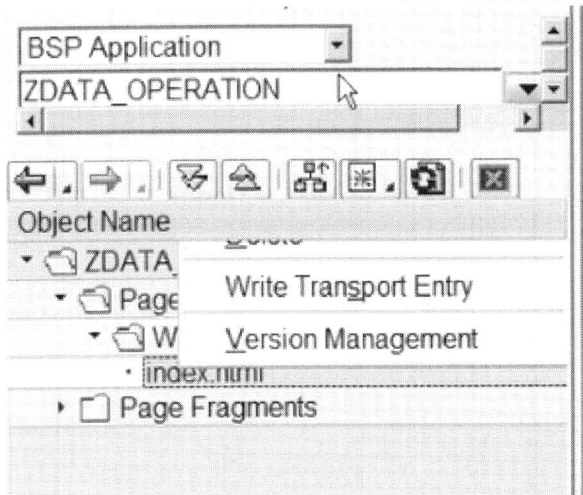

The default behaviour is opening the Internet Explorer.

Our Application is by default opening in Internet explorer(IE)

You can see some of the fields like client name, language and app caches, are appended at the end of the URL by default. If we copy the URL and performed used our chrome browser then you can see the same application running which we saw in localhost.

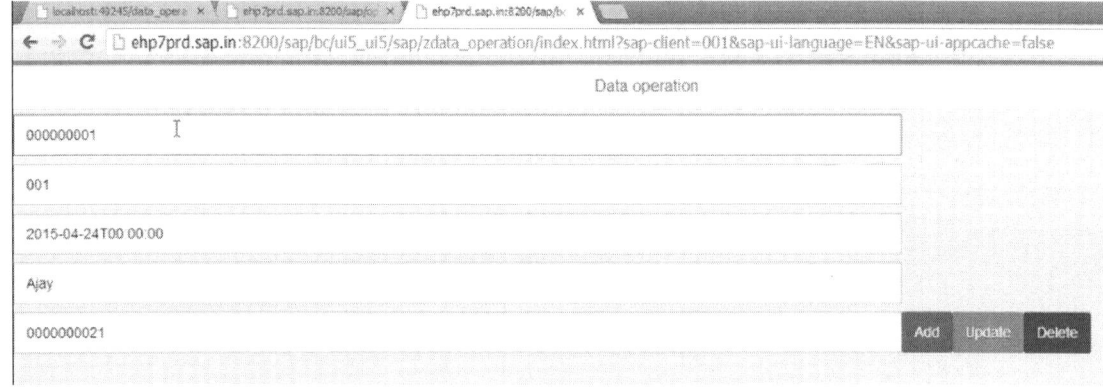

But in this case, we are inside this application which is running from SAP. We can perform the same step here as well to test our application which will work exactly the same way.

Summary

With this section, we came to the end of our SAP NetWeaver Gateway book.

In this book, we saw gateway implementation where gateway exists within our SAP backend. This model is also sometimes referred to as embedded deployment, and is the preferable model for learning gateway.

We saw CRUDQ operation from SAP UI5 application, and we came to know how the services we built in the previous section will be used by the front end developer in the SAP UI5 applications.

As these services are exposed as REST-based services, or specifically OData protocol-based services, they can be utilized in many other applications. If you are building an Android or a Java application, or even PHP applications, these services will be able to communicate, and do the exact work of giving data and executing operation in your SAP backend.

SAP UI5 already provides some of the libraries and classes which are going to be used by your front end developer team to make their life a lot easier. We also saw how they will be going to use those libraries.

After that, we saw how to push SAP UI5 application to SAP, how to launch the application from SAP into your browser, and how to use your application. That will be exactly how customers are going to use your application, but the difference is that they will be having a quick launch URL for your application instead of executing it from your object repository.

You can also, check our SAPNetweaver Gateway course which demonstrates all the above steps in simple and easy to understand manner.
for the course coupon click here or use the QR code.

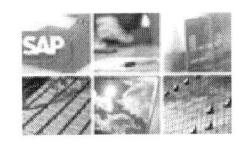

SAP Netweaver Gateway for SAPUI5, SAP Fiori and SAP HANA
UI5 Community Network , SAP Experts - SAP Services, SAP Consulting, SAP Education
20 € · ★★★★½ 4.2 (25 ratings) · 27 lectures, 3.5 hours video · All Levels

Printed in Great Britain
by Amazon